Look Back and Laugh!

Make your past funnier. Make your life healthier!

John Schmidtke

ISBN 978-1-63575-087-4 (Paperback)
ISBN 978-1-63575-088-1 (Digital)

Christian Faith Publishing, Inc.
296 Chestnut Street
Meadville, PA 16335
www.christianfaithpublishing.com

Printed in the United States of America

To my wife Diane, who taught me to love…
and still shows me how.

FOREWORD

Burdened by your past? Don't be.

Your past, the downs as well as the ups, can be a real blessing. It all depends on how you look at it. Laughter is the key. Whatever happened (ridiculous, riotous, or ruinous) happened. If you can laugh at it, you can live with it.

Of course, I'm not talking about especially dark events like death, terrible illness, awful accidents, crime, or abuse. I'm talking about misfortune, bad luck, embarrassment, or misunderstanding. The things that can make us blush or steam years later when they come back to visit in the dark of night.

As you will soon read, my wife Diane and I have had more than our share of potholes along the road of life. The craziness could have killed us. But we decided to laugh about it. The laughter changed our lives.

There is humor in everything. All you have to do is find it. Laughter is good medicine. too. When you think back on even a bad event with laughter, it will bring a smile instead of tears or anger. It'll help you—and everyone around you—because happiness is catchy.

That's why I wrote this book. I want you to look back and laugh. To learn how to think about the past and laugh instead of cry.

Everything in this book is true. I just want you to see it the way I see it… now. Read along and see how it's done.

Then try it yourself. Pretty soon, there will a happier person smiling back at you in the mirror.

CHAPTER 1

An Upside-Down Introduction!

I put myself through college at Northern Illinois University. I was the first one in my entire extended family to actually go to college, let alone try to graduate.

I saved for years. I worked double shifts at the local steel mill in the summer. Then during the school year, I worked in the cafeteria kitchen. Forty hours a week and a full load of classes. Now for a blue-collar guy like me, it was no sweat working on the dish washing machine. No, wait a minute. There was plenty of sweat!

The dish room was always hot from the steam in the dishwasher. But if there was a job I loved—and I mean really loved—it was loading the dishwasher. Loading up the moving rack—just like the one in your dishwasher—which moved along a conveyer inside the dishwasher until it came out the other end. I'd wait for a bunch of dishes, then deal them out just like a card dealer in Las Vegas. One after the other, row after row. By my sophomore year, I was the ace of aces. Nobody loaded dishes faster than me.

I've been out of school for decades, and I still load my dishwasher fast!

At the other end were two poor guys desperately trying to keep up. To be honest, their job was tougher. All I had to do was grab dishes, cups, glasses, silverware, and trays. Then I loaded them. Actually, I crammed them! I stuffed them into the machine as fast as I could. The more, the merrier. The faster, the better.

This got my job done right away. It also caused mayhem at the other end. Because, you see, it was all a game. At the other of the machine was a safety rack. Sort of a bumper. If a dish remained in the rack and hit the bumper, the machine would stop. It became my goal in life to stop that machine. It became the goal of life for the two poor souls on the other end to keep that machine going.

They had it rough. They not only had to take out the dishes but also put all of them in the right places. I took true joy in hearing the screams from the other end. The manager had a rather different reaction, especially to breakage. Sometimes, there would be three guys down there. You get the idea. This was my world and I was on top of it. I hadn't had a whole lot of success in life up to then (I still haven't, really), but I was lord of the cafeteria dish room.

That was me.

This was her.

Diane became the love of my life. Unfortunately, I didn't know it yet. She was this lovely freshman girl who worked out front on the serving line. Where it was pleasant, cool, nice. For some reason known only in heaven, she took a liking to me. But alas, fate seemed destined to keep us forever apart.

She worked up front. I worked in back. She worked on the serving line and smelled wonderful. I worked back in the dish room… and smelled. Let's just say that she was dry and I was wet. Not to mention the fact that she worked at the beginning when everybody was being served, and I worked at the end when everybody had been. Her dishes were clean until she put food on, and my dishes were dirty until I took food off.

Two different worlds.

There were other differences, which only goes to prove that opposites really do attract. If you get married later, then they drive you nuts. But at the beginning, opposites attract.

Really, though. We were different.

She had dated every boy at her high school, and most of them several times. The only dates I had were swimming meets that were on the calendar. She was from the north suburbs of Chicago—white collar; I was from the south suburbs—blue collar. If you're familiar with the Chicago area, you know that means a lot more than just geography.

Her dad was a sales executive. My dad was a steelworker.

So. What to do? What to do?

Nothing if not resourceful, Diane decided to make the first move. It's taken me decades to realize that most women do that!

One afternoon, she got her chance. The manager came up to me with these dreaded words. "We're short some people tonight. We need you to mop the floor out in the serving area."

I was not impressed. I was lord of the dish room. That night alone, I had stopped the dish washing machine three times. Everything was going great. Why ruin things now? "I wash dishes," I said. "I don't do floors."

"Well, you do tonight," she said. "Or at least, you better do it tonight."

So there I was, dragging my bucket through the kitchen, glumly mopping the floor. Head down, whispering to myself. Recalling my glory time in the dish room with my beloved dishwashing machine.

I wasn't really paying much attention to anything or anybody around me. I was concentrating on the floor. Doggone it, if I could make dirty dishes clean fast, then I could sure make a dirty floor clean. Fast. Swish, swish-push, push-pull, pull. At the rate I was going, I'd have won the Indy 500. Unfortunately, this job seemed like an endless pit stop.

The manager knew I wasn't too thrilled about this project so she came out to see how I was doing. I pushed the mop out and talked with her for a minute. I explained how wonderful it was to have an opportunity to contribute to the well-being of all mankind and make my contribution to world peace by mopping the kitchen floor. Or words to that effect.

When she was safely out of sight, I let it all hang out. I yanked on the mop to get going again.

How was I to know that this lovely freshgirl was standing on my mop?

When I looked up, the first thing I saw—well, let's not talk about the first thing I saw! Let's just talk about the fact that it was four feet up in the air!

My first thought was awful. "Oh my gosh, I'm going to have to tell this girl's father that I killed her with a mop!" It would have been quite a phone call. "Hello, sir. My name is John. I just wanted to call and let you know I got your daughter high here at college… literally." I'm sure he would have understood, maybe.

What could I do? I picked her up. She was laughing through the pain. I asked if we could go to the next basketball game… if she could walk. She could. And we did.

Marriage came later. But this was the only time I can ever remember her slipping up!

I couldn't believe she could fall down like that and get up looking great. She's still good at it!

CHAPTER 2

My Never-before-Heard Prayer

Diane was a believer. She had been raised in a nice church. She knew her Bible completely and believed everything in it.

I wasn't a believer. I was an attender. I was raised in a mainline church, never had opened a Bible, and didn't understand anything in it. You could probably say that I really didn't know anything spiritual but was vaguely suspicious. Vaguely.

There we were, both in college. She didn't like the church I was attending, and I never heard of hers. We made a deal to go to my church on Sunday morning and her church on Sunday night. That seemed all right with her.

Diane got excited when my church announced special Wednesday night services all during Lent. Her church at home met on Wednesday nights too. They also had services on Sunday night! *Wow*, I thought. *Do they live at church? Why would you want to spend that much time at church? Do you have to be eternal to be immortal?*

What really excited her was the speaker.

The visiting pastor was in his seventies. In the years before World War 1, he had traveled all through Northern Illinois to plant new churches for the denomination. Now he was retiring and had decided to preach in each of those churches. The Lenten services in my church were our congregation's turn.

Right away, I noticed something different. Those older preachers were big on the Bible, even the guys from mainline denomina-

11

tions. They wanted people to really commit to Jesus Christ. Decide. Now. Instantly if not sooner. I had never heard anything like that from my home team! I listened and learned.

Then one night, he concluded with a story:

A young man was born into a wonderful family. He was raised right. His parents were well-to-do and he had every advantage. But he squandered it all on riotous, sinful living, drunkenness, and petty crime. Time and time again, he was arrested. The local judge so admired the family that he kept letting the son off.

But one day, the crime was so terrible and the son was so guilty, the judge had to sentence the young man to prison.

There in his cell, the son thought things over. *I'm nuts*, he thought. *I had every advantage. I had a good home. I had a good upbringing. Yet here I am in prison for doing something really bad.*

The son decided to write home. He wrote, "I'll be getting out of jail soon. I'd like to come home on the train. But I know I've embarrassed you and ruined the family name. Could I come home? The train tracks run right by your property. There's a big tree there. If you want me to come home, would you please hang a white handkerchief on the tree? If I see it, I'll come home. But if there is nothing on the tree, I'll understand and just stay on the train."

A real prodigal son.

The big day came. He got on the train. Along the way, he shared his story with the man sitting next to him by the window. Finally, he said, "There's a big tree on your side of the car. It's right around the curve. Would you please tell me if there is a white handkerchief hanging on it?"

The train went around the bend. The son sat with his head in his lap, his hands over his eyes. He was too afraid to even look.

But everyone in the train started to laugh and applaud. The man sitting there said, "Look at this, young man! You've got to see this for yourself!"

The son looked. And there was the tree. His father had hung everything white he owned on the tree. Bed sheets, white shirts, tablecloths, towels, underwear, socks. Everything. Then the son knew he was loved. He knew he could come home.

That's when the old mainline preacher seemed to look me right in the eye.

"That's how much God loves you. You personally. The father didn't love the son with just a handkerchief. He loved him with everything white he had!"

"God loves *you* that much! Think about it. You're on the train of your life. You're on track to the future. But along the way, you wonder. Does God love me? Would God want me in heaven?"

"Then you look out the train window of your life and you see how much Your Heavenly Father loves you. He loves you so much that He hung everything of value He has on the tree. He hung His son Jesus Christ there to prove it."

I sat there stunned. Suddenly, all the Sunday school lessons I ignored or never understood made sense.

The preacher asked, "If God loves you that much, will you get off the train of your life and accept the love God has for you? Will you commit your life to Him?"

He invited us to come forward after the service if that was what we wanted. It was what I wanted.

In my church back home, the pastor always walked down the aisle to the foyer after the service to greet everyone. If this pastor would have tried that, I would have tackled him.

He stayed in front. I came up and talked with him. He asked if we could pray together. We did. He asked if I wanted to commit my life to Christ. I did.

Then he asked, "Is there anything else you'd like to pray?"

I said, "Yes." And I prayed an eight-word prayer.

The pastor looked at me with wide eyes. "In all of my fifty years of ministry, I've never heard a prayer like that. Please tell me what it means."

Here was my prayer: "Lord, give me a real good right now."

It was easy for me to explain. All my life, I had wanted to be someone else, to be somewhere else, and most important, to have been born at some other time. I'd wanted to have been born a hundred years before and fight in the Civil War or battle with wild Indians. Or hundred years into the future and fly around in space ships with Flash Gordon or Buck Rogers. But not born where and when I was actually born, in Chicago in the 1940s.

I was spending all my life regretting the past or fearing the future. So I asked God for a real good right now.

I knew I couldn't control my temper for the rest of my life, but I could control it right now. I knew I couldn't always be the best I could be, but I could be the best I could be right now. I might have doubts about every spiritual thing I knew, but I could believe right now.

He smiled. "That's a wonderful prayer," he said. "I think I'll pray it myself!"

CHAPTER 3

An Unsightly Honeymoon…

The happiest day of my life was when Diane and I were married. My attitude that day was the same as when we first met. I couldn't understand why a woman so nice could fall in love with a guy like me.

But she did. And does. So there we were on Easter morning, driving to church. I had hidden an engagement ring in my Bible. I asked about a particular verse, and Diane looked it up in her Bible. She found it right away, like always, and read it to me. I pulled off the road for a second. "That's not what my Bible says," I said, opening it. The engagement ring was hidden inside. When I opened the Bible, there was the ring. "My Bible says, 'I love you. Will you marry me?'"

She said, "Yes!" She actually said, "Yes!" To me!

God is good… all the time! All the time, God is good!

The wedding was great. The banquet was fine. But like all guys, I was really looking forward to the first night of our honeymoon! We had waited for each other. And she was certainly worth the wait!

The next morning, we were ready to go out and have a wonderful time.

That's when she lost a contact lens (for the first time in her life!) in the deep white shag carpet. We hadn't even gotten to breakfast. We looked and looked and looked. I had both eyes. She had one. But we used all three.

She then spent the rest of our honeymoon walking around like a barbary pirate, one hand over her eye. Personally, I thought she

15

looked fantastic. She said I looked good too, from what she could see of me.

Incredibly, we decided to come home early. We actually checked out of the hotel and came home early!

Why not? We wanted to get started with our new life. Diane needed a new contact lens. And I, being a guy, figured we could just as easily do what we wanted to in our apartment... for free.

We did all three. Came home early, started out our new life together, and had a blast in our apartment.

Love is blind. Or at least it was! Really.

CHAPTER 4

Four Days of Labor, One Kid...

When we got married, we didn't know much about sex. Actually, we didn't know anything about sex!

But we must have been doing something right because Diane got pregnant right away. Immediately. Let's just say she never completed the first sentence. No period!

The funny thing is, we lived in a four-unit apartment building. All four couples used the same birth control method from the local drugstore. All four couples got pregnant immediately. Now that I think about it, I'm sure the local obstetrician bribed the drugstore to carry this item.

Our first baby came nine months and seventeen days after our wedding.

For most of that time, I was nervous. Not for her condition. For our reputation.

"Don't have this baby early," I said. "We waited until our honeymoon like everyone said we should. If this baby comes early, we're going to have to do an awful lot of explaining to a whole bunch of friends and relatives!" So for nine months, I was nervous. After that, I was fine.

It was the longest nine months and the shortest seventeen days of my life!

After nine months passed, everything was okay with me! "Go skip rope!" I said. "Buy a pogo stick! Play hopscotch!"

Soon thereafter, the labor started. We were both nervous. We knew less about childbirth than we did about sex. And that's saying a lot! Or a little!

We drove to the hospital and Diane was admitted. After a few hours, the labor pains stopped. After a few more hours, when they didn't start again, Diane was discharged. Home we went.

We were disappointed, but I was sort of glad. We had spent the weekend at the hospital but at least I could go back to work Monday on my still-new job.

So, of course, the labor started again real early Monday morning. I called in to work and got ready for us to go back to the maternity ward. The only problem was Diane didn't want to go. At least not yet. "I'm not going back there unless I can come home with a baby!" she said.

Doggone it; that sounded reasonable! Scary, but reasonable.

So there at home we sat, her feeling the pain, me staring at the clock. She thought I was timing the pains. I was actually wondering when work started.

But those pains! Harder and harder. I'm not usually the one to get nervous. I pretty much leave that up to Diane. But it came down to her determined not to go too early. And me determined not to go too late!

As you can imagine, the pains made the decision for us. Off we went a second time.

Before I tell you too much more, I need to tell you that the hospital maternity ward was being remodeled. The whole place was torn up. The hallway was dark. Lights were strung everywhere. It was an interesting environment, especially when a woman down the hall would start to scream.

I became immediately impressed with the wide range of vocabulary some women possess. Some were using all of it. I thought having a baby was supposed to be joyful. Those women didn't seem to know that yet.

Since then, women have told me that having a baby is like going to the bathroom and trying to pass a watermelon.

What an interesting thought. Delicious perhaps, but certainly interesting.

Anyway, the place looked like a cave. It sounded like a cave. It felt like a cave.

There we sat. Waiting. Timing the labor pains. Waiting. For hours. Meeting new nurses as the shifts changed. Waiting for something magical called "dilation." I didn't know much about it, but it had something to do with fingers. For whatever reason, Diane didn't have enough fingers. She had five on each hand (including the thumbs), but not enough fingers someplace else.

One day. Two days. Three days. Meanwhile, back at the office, the guys started asking, "Who's having the baby—her or him?"

By now, Diane was wearing some kind of belt, which measured the strength of each labor pain. Ever helpful, I would look at the dial and let her know how strong the pain was. She didn't really need or much appreciate the information.

Eventually—thankfully, mercifully—the fingers of fate happened. And my wife—this lovely little girl, as gentle as anyone I had ever met—proceeded to rip the wristwatch off my arm. With a lot of hair. I was amazed. In pain, too.

Baby making is fun. Baby getting? Not so much. Later maybe. Not right then.

It was time for me to leave. In those days, believe it or not, no one was in the delivery room except the mother and the medical people. Nowadays, it's almost like people read a page from the phonebook and invite everybody.

Not us. Not me. I sat down the hall in the waiting room, trying to actually believe that I would be a father in a little while.

That's when I heard the scream. Not Diane, the baby! From all the way down the hall. Through two sets of double doors.

Wow! I thought. *I sure hope that's a boy!* It was.

He's all grown up now with children of his own. In his forties. In all that time, he still hasn't yelled as loud.

What a four days! It took a while, but we were on our way. One baby down, three to go.

CHAPTER 5

Little Kids and Questions

I know we're supposed to teach our children. And if we're good parents, we do. But little ones also teach *you* a lot.

Kids need to understand that parents *learn* to be parents. It's why we always say that the only thing you owe your first child is an apology.

It's not like there's a parenting license like there's a driving license or anything. Good thing. We'd all fail.

One especially nice thing is that children remind you of how fresh and exciting their world can be. Everything is new to them. There's no governor on their lips. There are no guardrails on their minds.

It's all new all the time.

Here's a good example. When Karl was still little, Diane sent us two out to pick up some groceries at the store. We had our list. When we got to the store, Karl was in the little seat in the shopping cart.

Here's another thing. There were no car seats in those days. No seat belts. No nothing. Yet all four of our kids survived. They actually reached adulthood, uninjured and relatively unscathed. I never thought twice about it. But I sure do now when I won't move the car until I tell the grandkids to buckle up! Can't be too careful.

Well, I digress. Back to the store where Karl and I were shopping. Eggs were on the list. So I got a carton of a dozen eggs and, like I always do, opened it and looked closely to see if any were broken.

Karl looked at me and asked, "Could I smell them too?"

Apparently, they smelled just fine. Not as good as when they are scrambled. But good enough.

They weren't cracked either.

Our daughter Gayle loved to ask, "How come it's such a beauty day?"

When Jeff was little, he dreamed up this beaut. "How come the sun only shines during the day when we got enough light, but never at night when it's dark and we can't see so good?"

Another time when we were out on the lake. "How come fish don't drown?"

Yet another time. "You know why Easter is my favorite time? 'Cause that's when Jesus dived off the cross…"

All I could think of was the Olympics with the announcer saying, "Jesus Christ of Nazareth. A quadruple, twisting gainer in the pike position. Difficulty ten point oh." He, of course, executes it perfectly.

He'd have gotten a perfect score, too, if not for the East German judge.

CHAPTER 6

How Everything Came
out with Gayle

God decided it was time for us to have another baby we couldn't afford.

The problem was not that Diane and I didn't know anything about sex or birth control. The problem we didn't even *suspect* anything!

While we waited for our baby's coming out party, I did a little thinking. We were going to be married for thirty-six months. Diane will have been pregnant for eighteen of them. "At this rate, we'll have over thirty kids on our fiftieth anniversary!"

Of course, there are things called menopause, sexual dysfunction, and sheer exhaustion; but I didn't know anything about those either.

But there was no doubt. Diane's "time of the month" had become her "time of the year!"

Knowing the big day was coming, I decided to take a paper route to make a little extra money. We were going to need it. Our health insurance was awful, and we were going to need money for all sorts of medical bills.

Unfortunately, I was out delivering newspapers when the big day came. I drove Diane over to her parents' apartment. The pains were coming pretty strong and fast.

But I had to go out in my car, throwing Sunday newspapers out the window onto driveways. To this day, I really believe that at least some of those newspapers were actually delivered to the right houses!

When I sped back to her parents' place, Diane was ready to leave. But not her mom. "John has to have some breakfast!" So she cooked up some scrambled eggs and toast for me.

That was great. My stomach was growling. But Diane's stomach was doing something quite a bit different.

Then we raced to the hospital. There we did what we did when our first baby had been born. We waited. And waited. And waited.

There were two would-be mothers in each room. We saw quite a few of them come and go. One woman really got to me. She and her husband were so calm. So quiet, so composed. Diane was in agony with intense labor pains. This woman was so nice and quiet. "Of my goodness, honey," she cooed to her husband. "This labor pain seems so strong… Feel my tummy." She was actually smiling when she said it.

"Oh yes, dear," he said, soothingly. "It certainly is…"

Soon, she was ready to go. Both as calm as a pond in summer, as quiet as a gentle breeze. They left before I could kill them. Off they went. Cool and collected.

There we stayed. Wild, wooly, and waiting.

Finally, I couldn't take it any longer. I asked Diane if I could step out into the stairwell for a second. She said it was fine.

I came back a few minutes later. The room was empty. An aide was remaking Diane's bed. "Where's my wife?" I asked, nervous as the dickens.

"Oh, she's not here anymore…"

Yikes, I thought. *'Not here' meaning not here in the room or 'not here' meaning no longer in the land of the living?*

I found out where she was. In the delivery room. Baby Gayle had decided to come out. Fast. Feet first fast. She hadn't even waited to turn around!

Actually, it wasn't feet first. Her legs were up by her head. I don't want to say what came out first but let's just say everyone knew she was a girl right away.

It took a few days before we could get her feet to lay flat for a nap.

This birth was better. Maybe Diane was getting the hang of it.

Four hours for the second one was way better than the four days for the first…

CHAPTER 7

The Great Garage Parade

We've always had a two and a half car garage whether we had a two and a half car garage or not. That is, we've always had two and a half cars worth of stuff in it even when our garage could barely hold a compact.

It was like that one time when the kids were little. Diane sent me out the door and said, "I understand there might be a concrete floor in the garage. Do you think you could clean up the garage a little bit and see if it's really true?"

Subtle hints like that get to me every time. "The kids will help you," she said. "It will be a good life lesson for them," she added. It's what Moms say when they need a little peace and quiet.

So, often, a husband's thoughts need to remain just that. Thoughts.

Off we went. The kids and I, into our garage. Well, we didn't actually go *into* the garage. It was too crowded in there. We just kind of stood in the driveway with the garage door open, staring. Then we—actually, I—started in. I threw out a bunch of stuff. I put a bunch of stuff up into the rafters. I hung a bunch of stuff on the walls.

There *was* a floor!

We weren't done, but the kids were really excited about the floor. Pretty soon they were doing what they had never stopped doing— playing. They asked me to play along. After working to clean the garage, I was extremely persuadable. "I got an idea!" I said, "Let's have a parade!"

Meanwhile, Diane was inside cleaning the house. When she happened to look out the front window, there we were. A parade, marching up and down the street. Singing our heads off.

The boys were holding shovels and rakes like rifles. The girls were waving rags as pom-poms. Pretty soon, neighbor kids joined in. It became a real circus. We had everything, even "wild animals" in wagons. They looked suspiciously like stuffed animals, but we knew they were real!

Diane thought it was great. She laughed and took pictures. Fortunately for me, she didn't go into the garage for a while.

The garage floor had re-disappeared.

CHAPTER 8

Dead Broke On the Mean
Streets of Chicago

I have to include this story because my wife will never let me forget it.

My wife and I have completely different concepts of money. Remember the old American Express commercial "Don't leave home without it"? That's Diane and money.

She has money crammed everywhere. In every purse. Scrunched up in every pocket. Every coat. Her life goal is to get as much money as possible crammed into the smallest possible space. I now volunteer to do laundry whenever I need a couple of bucks. I get plenty of cash she left behind. And I don't have to explain to her where I got it or what I intend to do with it.

Another thing is if, God forbid, she leaves this veil of tears before me, there is no way I will donate her clothes to charity until I go through every pocket. How else would I be able to pay for the funeral?

My concept of money is a little different. Completely opposite, in fact. It's probably based on the Bible verse "The love of Money is the root of all evil."

I almost avoid money. It has quickly departed from me all my life. They say, "A fool and his money are soon parted." I can personally attest to the truth of that. Both parts of the statement. The "fool" part *and* the "money" part.

Anyway, a big cause of conflict between us was my walking out the door without a dime in my pocket. Forget dimes. I walked out the door penniless, nickel-less, dimeless, quarterless, and dollar-less. Often, checkless too.

I might as well have pulled out all four pockets and walked around that way. It probably would have prevented me from being mugged. But it would also have prevented me from ever buying anything.

Which is a long way to get you to a short—but extremely embarrassing—story.

Almost right out of college, I got a nice job at a major drugstore chain. Part of my job was to frequent drugstores in Chicago to take photos or do interviews. All went well until once when I had to go right downtown. Of course, I parked my car in a public lot. Where else are you going to park in a big city?

However, unfortunately, you can't park for free.

I realized it when I went back to get my car. No cash. At the time, they didn't take a credit card. They wouldn't take a check either. Which didn't matter, since I hadn't brought my checkbook along.

So I had to go back to the drug store. I would have gone hat in hand… if I would have worn a hat.

I actually had to convince the manager that I really was an executive at headquarters. That the company actually *did* pay me a salary.

He was nice and lent me a couple of bucks to fetch my car. I returned it right away with a nice note.

It was an unforgettable lesson for me.

And even if it hadn't been, my wife would have made sure it stayed that way.

Unforgettable.

Now, the whole world knows…

CHAPTER 9

Those Darn Wise Guys

In Milwaukee, a lot of churches put on live nativity scenes at Christmas.

Diane and I were new to town and we'd never seen one. We heard about a church doing one and decided to go. We bundled up all four kids and piled into the car. We turned up the heat because it was cold, cold, cold.

Unfortunately, churches always put on their live nativity scenes at night. Not only is it colder at night, it even *seems* colder at night.

They also do it outside. It is *definitely* colder outside!

The first thing I noticed was that all the characters were bundled up in large coats under their costumes. The next thing I noticed was that all the actors were large. Apparently, this church considered potluck dinners a sacrament. The only small person was the doll of the baby Jesus.

Anyway, the Christmas story was told over the loudspeaker. You really don't realize how long it is until you listen to it and can't feel your feet.

It went on and on. I love the story, but golly. The trip to Bethlehem, the inn that was full, the stable, the star, the shepherds.

And, at last, finally, the wise men.

Unfortunately, these were the biggest, meanest-looking wise men we'd ever seen. They were wearing big coats under their robes. And they were moving slow. They had to because you can't move fast wearing three pairs of pants. Under the robes, of course. Slowly, they lumbered up to the manger.

Our son Jeff was only three at the time.

He took one look at the wise guys and whispered this memorable statement: "Don't let them steal my mittens."

We didn't. But we still laugh about it.

It's amazing how funny things can be after you thaw out.

CHAPTER 10

Peed Off at the TV Set

Karl was our first. He was a great baby, and it wasn't long before he was potty-trained. He couldn't wait to wear "big boy pants" all the time.

We explained the toilet. How to flush it. How to always lift up the seat before he went. "Remember, Karl, always lift the toilet seat before you go."

I saw a sign once, posted in a bathroom by a harried mom. "We aim to please. You aim, too, please!"

A great kid. Great teaching. Great results. Right?

Well, we went out for an evening and got a babysitter. The sitter was responsible. Karl was already asleep. There wouldn't be any problem.

Unfortunately, Karl woke up because he had to go. He wandered into the living room where our babysitter was watching TV. He came over to the TV, which had a volume control that was an up-and-down lever.

He flipped it up to maximum volume and, before the sitter could do anything, peed all over the screen!

The sitter was horrified. She explained that she'd cleaned it all up. Karl had just wandered off and gone back into the bedroom to go back to sleep. I told the sitter, "Don't worry, honey. It's all right."

We definitely gave her a couple of bucks extra that night!

Besides, I thought to myself, *Given some of the programs today, I've actually thought of doing that myself.*

Just saying, of course.

CHAPTER 11

My Worst Word Choice Ever

I was a pastor for years. I'm still an ordained minister. I've had a lot of shaky moments. But my most embarrassing moment in church came long before I became a minister.

I was asked to teach an adult Sunday school class. The topic was the church. It's one of my favorite subjects. I studied long and hard. Prepared diligently. Went over my notes time and again.

I had definite opinions about the church (the overall Christian church as well as each individual congregation). I believe the church is not the building. It's the people. It's not stained glass. It's stained lives who were washed clean. It's not about sitting on the premises. It's about standing on the promises.

Church also has a lot of problems. I remember an old poem I heard:

> To live above with the saints we love,
> Oh, won't that just be glory!
> But to live below with the saints we know,
> Well, that's a different story!

Anyway, the church is a big subject. But I was ready. And so was the audience. The interest was so great that we actually held the class in the sanctuary instead of a classroom.

I was at my best. I covered everything.

For my conclusion, I was emphasizing that the church is people. It's alive. It's literally the Body of Christ. It's not just an organization or group. It's a living thing.

And so I said... I really said...

"Friends, the church is not an organization... it's an orgasm!"

Dead silence.

Well, church IS exciting. But it's actually an "organism."

I'll never forget the two older ladies sitting in the back. Their faces told it all. Afterward, one said, "I don't know what he was talking about but it sure sounds exciting!"

They didn't ask me to teach much for a good long while...

CHAPTER 12

She Took the Other Car

Whenever my wife backs up the car, I'm reminded of one of those people with dark sunglasses and a white cane. She doesn't really use her eyes. It's more like using a compass. She picks a general direction and goes there. Zigzaggedly. Usually this isn't a problem. Our driveways were wide.

Wide enough, usually. Except this one time.

We had often talked about paneling our family room. Unfortunately, I was as good with paneling as I am with brain surgery. Which is, not at all. But my friend Vince knew what he was doing. He offered to come help.

This particular Saturday seemed like a good time. Diane had signed up for a Christian women's conference. She was leaving early. So Vince and I would have the whole morning and probably most of the day to put up the paneling. All I had to do was help put up paneling and actually change diapers. Not necessarily in that order.

I really appreciated Vince helping. One of my personal confirmations that Jesus is truly God is that He was a carpenter. I think anybody who can do carpentry is pretty close to deity. Certainly unusual.

We got started early. Diane watched us put up the first few panels. As soon as she was convinced the house would still be standing when she got back, she left for the conference. It was snowing like crazy so I asked her to please be careful.

But right away—in just a few minutes—she came back and opened up the door a crack. "I think I'll take the other car," she said. "Terrific... okay," I said. "I'll drive the other one."

Then she was gone. Actually, I was glad. The car she took was better. It was newer. The snow was pretty bad. I thought she would be more safe.

Vince and I worked and worked. It took a while but finally the paneling was done. It looked great. We had skipped lunch. So I decided to run up to a fast food place and get something. Imagine my surprise when I walked out the door and saw our car in the front ditch! Our neighbor across the street came out. Ralph was laughing. He had never seen anything like it.

Well, sort of. The previous summer, he was sitting in his living room and watched my wife pull into our driveway. She got out of the car and walked into the house. Unfortunately, she turned off the car with the transmission in neutral. In that car, being in neutral meant it was free to roll.

While Ralph sat there in his living room, he watched our car go all the way down our driveway, across the street, onto *his* driveway... and hit his car! All the time, he was yelling, "John! John! What are you doing?"

For some reason, he thought I was driving. Maybe he thought I had dropped Diane off so I could go somewhere else. Me? I was— and still remain—innocent. I was downtown at work at the time.

Events like this are why car insurance agents love us. But that was last summer.

Another time, back when we first came to Milwaukee, Diane pulled into a neighbor's driveway and got out to walk into the house—but left the car running—in drive. Being obedient, the car kept going and rammed into the car in their garage.

Thankfully, their garage door was open. However, there was damage. I had the disheartening responsibility to call our car insurance agent and ask if our car was covered if it hit another car while nobody was driving. I was relieved to find out it *was* covered. Maybe that's why they call it *auto* insurance.

It was also nondrinker's insurance. After this one, I thought the agent might begin to have doubts. I suppose there's a big difference if you are drunk when you drive as opposed to when you drive like a drunk. But I'll have to ponder that one.

But that was years ago. My car was in our ditch now.

Ralph, still laughing, said, "If I didn't know you guys don't drink, I would've swore she was looped. The car weaved from side aside all the way down the driveway and ended up in your ditch."

Being the good neighbor he was, he hooked our car up to his truck and pulled it out. Ralph was a wonderful guy, a marine who fought on Iwo Jima during World War Two. He didn't talk much about combat.

With neighbors like us, why bother?

CHAPTER 13

A Hot Dog Named Charcoal

Getting a dog seemed like a good idea.

We had just moved into a new house. The kids were the right ages. Still little, but able to treat a dog well. We had a nice big lot. Best of all, the dog was cute... and free. She was a mixed breed like you wouldn't believe. Probably had 57 strands of DNA. A Heinz 57. But free. All positives, right?

Things got off to a good start. We trained the dog. She was jet-black, so we named her Charcoal. Even as a puppy, she was as friendly as the dickens. Everything changed one day when I took the kids outside to clean up the back yard. Naturally, they brought Charcoal along.

The kids were picking up branches. I was raking up leaves. *Hey,* I thought. *This is going well!*

Then my son Karl came over to me with some news. "Dad, Charcoal got a wire in her mouth and she won't let go."

That did *not* sound good. It seems the previous owners had removed an outdoor grill but left live wires exposed on the ground. Poor charcoal had them in her mouth and she was convulsing.

There was a whole lot of shakin' going on.

I grabbed her and pulled the wire out to the side. You could literally see the sparks in her teeth. The poor thing was staggering all around.

I didn't know what to do. "Get in the house!" I yelled to the kids. I went in too. I got on the phone right away to call the humane society. What in the world do you do with an electrified dog?

Who knew what a supercharged dog might do? I wanted the kids inside to keep them safe. So naturally, they opened up the back door to let her in.

I was trying to sound sane to the nice lady at the humane society, all the while yelling at the kids to stay away from the poor dog. Charcoal staggered around for a good while, wagging her tail but not knowing why. She would have failed every sobriety test known to man. Eventually, she came out of it. We loved her up.

Needless to say, things were never the same.

Charcoal was apparently fried between the ears. She lost all sense of place. She didn't know here from there. She forgot where she lived.

She not only had no train of thought, she didn't even have a caboose!

Therefore, she ran away constantly. Our back screen door didn't quite latch, and she perfected the technique of crashing through it and taking off whenever and wherever she liked.

Our neighbors called constantly. "Your dog is in our yard… again."

"Your dog is pooping on our front lawn… again."

"Your dog is digging a hole in our grass… again."

If speed dial had existed back then, we'd have been on it.

Our relationship with Charcoal is probably where the phrase "love-hate relationship" came to be.

After a while—actually, after about a dozen "whiles"—Diane got a little tired of running around the neighborhood in her robe, sobbing, sweating—calling to the dog.

She said it was either her or the dog. Making the decision didn't take as long as I thought it might. Between Charcoal and me, one of us still had a brain. I'm pretty sure it was me.

We took Charcoal to the Humane Society in our county. Paid a fee to have them accept her. Problem solved, right?

Well, it would have been solved if Diane hadn't called the Humane Society a week later. It turns out that if an older dog isn't claimed after a week, the dog is put to sleep. My wife, bless her heart, couldn't stand the thought. So believe it or not, she had us go back and actually pay $75 to readopt Charcoal.

When we got home, Charcoal celebrated by running out the back screen door and taking off across the field. I found her that night.

As days went on, she occasionally stopped by the house for food and water. On one of those visits, we realized she was pregnant.

When she finally delivered, it was a great educational experience for our kids. I have to admit it was a special thing to see.

Eight puppies. All different colors. All different sizes. All different shapes. Our veterinarian estimated eight different fathers. I think it may have been more like fifty. There were an awful lot of happy male dogs wagging their tails in our subdivision.

Now, the big question. Which puppy would we keep? I took this responsibility seriously. After all, my wife's sanity was on the line. Mine too.

I put all eight puppies into a little group. I stood about ten feet away and called, "Come!" One little black fuzz ball staggered over to me, wagging its tail. I put them all back in the same group and said the same thing. The same little puppy staggered over. The choice was made.

That was Piper, the best dog we ever had.

We named her after our daughter's best friend in school. It was an honor we never shared with the poor girl. Having a grandchild named after you is one thing… but a dog?

The rest of the story was predictable, but memorable. We had to take Charcoal and the rest of the puppies to a *different* humane society. Neither one of us had the guts to take her back to the previous one!

Because Diane thought it might be difficult for me to get rid of Charcoal and the puppies, she invited a friend to ride along with me over to the pound.

When we got back, the friend commented to her that I must be a pretty hard case. "I couldn't believe it!" he said. "John was actually *singing* all the way to the pound! I thought he'd be sad…"

After she was able to stop laughing—it took about twenty minutes—she explained the cause of my ecstasy.

Then we had hot dogs for dinner.

CHAPTER 14

The Time Santa Snuck In

When the kids are little, it's the question you always dread. "Dad, is there really a Santa Claus?"

What do you say to that?

"Right, kid, Mom and I have been lying to you all these years." But I couldn't do that. Karl was the oldest. We had three more right behind him who were absolutely certain Santa is real. To them, no Santa meant no presents.

So like any good dad, I tried to weasel out of it. Besides, we had a system. At our house, Santa came on Christmas Eve. So we would work out some way to get the kids out of the house. Then I'd run in to wherever the gifts were hidden and spread them all out under the tree. Then we'd leave for dinner or something and come back to the big surprise.

Unfortunately, Karl had figured it all out.

"C'mon, Dad. Every year, you put us all in the car and then mom tells you to go back in because you forgot to do something. You're in the house for a while. I think that's when you put out all the gifts. There's no Santa, Dad. Right, Dad? All my friends say so."

"Oh yeah?" I said, feeling like someone being interrogated by Perry Mason (for the younger among us, he was a television lawyer). "I don't know, Karl. You might be right."

I made up my mind to somehow come out on top for this one.

So a few days before Christmas, I walked over to our nice neighbor Paul and explained the whole thing. I gave him a key to the house and told him where all the Christmas presents were hidden. I asked him to put them all under the tree while we were out and then make tracks.

When Christmas Eve came, we piled into the car and started to pull away. Karl was shocked. "Dad, didn't you forget something?" He glanced over at his sisters and brother. "Dad, there was nothing under the tree."

"I know, son. What restaurant should we go to?"

We had a nice dinner. Karl was a little quiet for him. But everything went well.

And, lo and behold, when we got home, there were all the presents piled under the tree! The little ones were thrilled like always. Karl wasn't. At least, he was a lot quieter than usual. He looked like he wanted to check out the locks on all the windows and doors.

Later, when I came into his room to say prayers, he let it all out. He was actually crying. Scared to death. He said, "Dad, if a fat old guy like that can break into our house, we'll never be safe again!"

I wasn't expecting that.

So I had to explain the whole thing. My plot was completely unraveled. "Look, son. I had to do something. I didn't want you to ruin Christmas for the other kids. So Paul and I pulled this stunt to fool you."

Now Karl actually *was* happy. "That was a great joke, Dad."

"And, Dad, don't worry. I won't tell anyone..."

Terrific, son. Now I've written it in a book!

CHAPTER 15

Hugging the Wrong Leg

Daughters aren't fair. I think it's that way for all fathers. I had never been wrapped around such a tiny finger in my whole life.

Both our daughters fit that mold, especially our youngest daughter Keri. She adored her dad. She'd sit there and just stare at me. One of my favorite things was when she would come over to where I was sitting and just hug my leg. A big, big hug, with both arms holding tight. Then she'd look up at me with those big eyes.

It almost made me forget the dirty diapers. Almost.

Once, when she got a little older, our church decided to have a father-daughter kite fly. It was simple. Just bring a kite out to the parking lot and fly it with your daughter. It doesn't sound like much, but it was a blast. The little girls were all so excited to be doing something fun with dad.

Pretty soon, the parking lot was wild and wooly with the girls running all over the place. Naturally, we dads were doing all the kite-flying. We were talking with each other, always keeping a wary eye on the kite.

After a while, my friend Bill quietly called over to me. "John, what's this all about?"

There was Keri, hugging his leg with all her might.

Bill and I both had brown pants on.

It didn't take long for things to sink in with Keri. She never had actually looked up at Bill. She just looked over at me. You could see her thought process. "Wait a minute. That's my dad over there. I'm over here. WHO'S LEG AM I HUGGING?"

Then she looked up in horror, saw Bill looking down, and broke the sound barrier running over to me. She actually blocked the circulation in my leg for a while.

Bill and I were laughing. He said, "John, my own kids don't even hug me like that! Count your blessings!"

I did. I still do. All four of them. And all eighteen of the blessings *they* have!

When Keri got just a little older, I turned it into a lesson. "Honey, some people love the wrong things in this world. They hold onto them and never let go. They don't realize that God has something much better. In fact, God Himself is much better. You should love Him as much as you can."

God still is. And she still does.

CHAPTER 16

It's a Real Hit When I Drive

Lest you think Diane is the only one who has troubles with cars, I have to confess to also be a member of the "bumper car" club.

Over the years, I finally figured out why there's a windshield in the front *and the back* of the car. It's helpful—and safer and less expensive—to use both.

When our son Karl was in college in Texas, he was given a ride home in his friend's truck. His friend stayed with us and left his truck in our driveway. The truck was pretty new and, just to be safe, he parked it well down the driveway and on the other side from where I would pull out to go to work.

It was a great plan. And a nice truck. Until I slammed into it the next morning.

Before I left, Diane warned me. "Don't forget about the truck in the driveway!" Then she tried to go back to sleep. It's tough to do that when you hear a car crash in your driveway.

You see, I was being especially careful. She Who Must Be Obeyed had warned me. I was backing up using the rearview mirror on the driver's side. But the truck was on the right side of the driveway. I never saw it. But I definitely found it.

In addition to a really interesting-looking bumper, there was another problem. The boys were going back to college in a few days. They needed the truck.

I wasn't too worried about our cars. Our cars generally double in value every time we fill up the gas tank. His truck—his nice truck—was a different story.

Fortunately, Diane is a wonderful cook. She made a deal with our body shop friend that if he would repair the car quickly, we'd pay him with real money *and* a nice apple pie. If you'd ever taste Diane's pies, you know this is a deal you can't refuse!

I never contacted our insurance agent about this one. I can't imagine why.

Actually, we probably *should* have called him. He had gotten to know us quite well. On a first-name basis, in fact.

CHAPTER 17

Gayle's Sign Language

We attended a nice church. It was already big, but they were always encouraging more people to come. We met new people every Sunday.

One Sunday, a young mother came up to us and said, "What a wonderful church this is! I know this is where God wants us to be! My son is deaf. He says he found a nice little girl just like him! Is that your daughter over there?"

Sure enough, there was Gayle, using sign language with this woman's son. They were signing at warp speed. Both laughing. The little guy was thrilled.

The mother knew sign language, of course. She was watching Gayle. "Your daughter is so nice! She's saying such wonderful things! We are so excited. We'll see you next week!"

Needless to say, Diane and I were flummoxed. Gayle had never used sign language in the house. She had never mentioned it. But there she was, as fluent as anyone we'd ever seen.

On the way home, we asked her about it. Then it all came out.

"Dad, it's like this. Our teacher watches us like a hawk. If she sees us passing a note, she comes to get it and reads it in front of the whole class. We were afraid to use notes any more. So we all learned sign language."

"Now, whenever teacher turns her back, we use sign language to talk. She never sees us and none of the boys know what we're saying!"

Now what in the world do you say to that? "Gayle, I'm so proud of you being able to make that little hearing-impaired boy feel welcome" or "Gayle, you should not be talking to each other in class even if you're not actually talking to each other in class."

The first sentence made more sense.

Gayle has gotten even better over the years. She has signed in a wonderful "silent choir." She's signed for the national anthem at professional baseball and football games. She's been on television.

Who says kids never learn anything at school!

CHAPTER 18

Gayle and Her Caterpillars

Our daughter Gayle was a nature lover, sort of.

She collected things, took photos, read about plants and animals. She and Mother Nature were pals.

One fall, she became fascinated with caterpillars. All those colors! All the different types and sizes!

So naturally, she decided to go out one Saturday and start a collection. I found a little box for her and off she went. I was amazed when she got back. She proudly opened the box and there they all were. I couldn't believe she actually was able to cram that many caterpillars into one box.

It was a New York City traffic jam for caterpillars.

She went off by herself to admire them all some more. After a while, I decided to explain to her that it wouldn't be good to keep them because their job was to transform themselves into beautiful butterflies.

I had thought up a real nice speech. All about how God can make us into whatever He wants us to be. We can be transformed into something beautiful just like caterpillars can become butterflies.

Billy Graham would have been proud. Unfortunately, he didn't get the chance.

Gayle was nowhere to be found. I discovered her downstairs watching a nature program on television. "Where are the caterpillars?" I asked, trembling a little inside. "Up in my room!" she called over her shoulder as she danced up the stairs.

Then came the bloodcurdling scream.

"They're gone! All of them are gone!"

She'd left the box open. We never did actually figure out how many potential butterflies were in that box. But it was plenty.

We also learned that caterpillars move fast, are creative, and aren't fussy. A few were easy to find. Others were in a variety of places. Up on curtains. Under the box spring. Under bed covers. In desk drawers.

In stacks of towels.

In clothes hanging in the closet (how did they get up there?). One time, I was putting on my suit coat and one actually flew out when I put my arm through the sleeve.

Behind furniture, inside furniture.

You name where, we found 'em there!

We found caterpillars—or their dearly departed remains—all winter.

I urged Gayle not to worry. She felt awful. I don't know if she felt awful about how much trouble she was causing, or awful that all her precious butterflies were gone. "It's all right," I said, faking my best loving, patient father voice.

"Forget about it."

So she did.

We couldn't. Too many reminders.

CHAPTER 19

My Formula for Teaching

Every once in a while, I got to teach adult Sunday school. I wasn't that good. It was just that our church wasn't that fussy.

One Sunday morning, I went through my lesson with the class. The Q and A session went well. I was pretty happy afterward.

I was careful not to appear too pleased or smug. I have trouble with pride. I always have.

You should hear my speech about humility. It's fantastic!

But anyway, I was pleased when a young mom came up afterwards and said, "I can't tell you how encouraged I was by you this morning."

"Really?" I said.

"Yes!" she said, beaming. "I saw the baby formula all down your pants leg and I knew you had the same kind of morning as me!"

I once heard an excellent definition of humility: "Humility is a completely accurate image of yourself—nothing more, nothing less."

That quote has terrified me ever since.

CHAPTER 20

South African Softball

Coaching girls' softball ain't easy. That's why so many people don't do it.

I, on the other hand, have a unique capacity to anticipate problems that could happen.

Like making sure your wife knows where the bathroom is when nature calls a little girl while she's batting.

Like making sure the real rookies run down the first base line and not the third baseline, a significant problem especially for lefties.

Like being able to find a pitcher on the team who can actually lob the ball somewhere near the plate. Needless to say, the umpires have a significantly expanded strike zone. But there's nothing you can do when the ball doesn't even roll near the plate.

These problems were relatively minor because, fortunately, the coach of the other team was usually facing the same set of obstacles.

Except for one year.

On my team were three triplets from South Africa.

They were cute, bubbly, happy, excited… and completely—and I mean completely—ignorant of softball.

I became suspicious as I was trying to explain the rules. I stood at home plate and pointed to the both baselines. "A ball that lands over here is fair. A ball that lands outside these lines is foul." Sounded good. Basic, but good.

After that, I was prepared to continue my brilliant discourse when all three asked in unison, "Why?"

It was like that for almost the whole season. "Wear the glove on this hand and throw with the other one."

"Why?"

"Stand on the base you're on or they'll tag you out."

"Why?"

"Hold the bat on the narrow end."

"Why?"

I must admit, I had fun that year. First of all, no one expected us to do well. And they were right.

Everyone admired me for my patience when the other team had the bases loaded with two outs and our South African right fielder was out there doing cartwheels.

They also admired my cool when the girls were playing infield. They couldn't catch anything, but all three of them used their feet to mark out a nice little rectangle in front of them. Finally, I called time and asked, "Why are you making those little boxes in the dirt?"

"Oh." They smiled. "We're marking out our space. If the ball comes in here, we have to catch it."

The umps didn't allow a long-enough timeout for me to properly address that issue.

All the parents (on both teams!) appreciated not having to stay too long at the game since the league's twenty-run mercy rule usually happened by the second or third inning.

My biggest frustration came late in the season when I saw all three girls playing soccer with a softball. They kicked it all over the field, passed it flawlessly to each other, played endlessly juggling the softball with their feet with it never hitting the ground.

I watched in amazement. Pele would have been proud. All three triplets have probably had professional soccer careers by now.

"Why didn't you girls go out for soccer?"

"Oh, soccer is too boring. Softball is way more fun!"

Gosh, they were right. Soccer is ridiculous. All those players running so much and playing so hard. Up and down the field. Up and down the field. Up and down the field. Up and down the field. With the game ending in a tie.

Now I know why soccer fans riot. They're not mad. They're frustrated!

Looking back, I now understand the South African triplets—and appreciate them—a whole lot more.

And, by the way, in the last game of the season, one of them actually got a hit. And she ran the right way, to first base.

Where she was later tagged out. When she wandered off the base.

But still. It was a hit! Even in South Africa, it would have been a hit!

She got a standing ovation. From me.

CHAPTER 21

When I Went Food Shopping for Our Camping Trip

I don't shop well. Which is why I usually am not sent to shop at all. Especially for food. I brought the right things home once. I think it was 1973. That's about it.

This one time, we were taking another one of our spur-of-the-moment camping trips. Diane had a list and was doing all the packing. She gave me the shopping list for food. "Come right back," she said. "I'm going to need your help!"

I took off for the grocery store. I hit a wall when I got inside. Not an actual wall. An intellectual wall. The list made absolutely no sense. Ever vigilant and always obedient, I pressed on.

Number one on the list. Pancakes.

Where in the store do you go to buy pancakes? Apparently, there's not a huge demand because I couldn't find any. After fifteen minutes or so, I decided frozen waffles were good enough. They would have to be. It was a big list.

The next item. Fried chicken. No sweat. I got a rotisserie chicken. It didn't make much sense to get one already cooked when we were going camping to cook one. But I always aim to please.

But my aim wasn't too good. The next one was mashed potatoes. Mashed potatoes! I had to ask for help. The closest even the clerk could come was a mashed potato mix. I happen to know Diane hates mashed potato mix. I assumed she wanted this for convenience of some sort.

Next item. Scrambled eggs. What's wrong with regular eggs? We could scramble them later. But the clerk decided what Diane really wanted was egg mix (which is a lot like the mashed potato mix except, of course, it's eggs!).

I was getting tired now. The clerk was tired of helping me. Now you have to remember, this was before cell phones. In those days, you actually had to think for yourself. Or at least try to.

Next on the list. Texas Sheet Cake. Texas Sheet Cake! There wasn't any of that anywhere. And this was a big store. There was, however, a chocolate cake. It was fairly big. Texas is fairly big. Close enough.

This wasn't getting any easier. I'd been there for almost two hours. Next on the list was baked bean casserole. That did it. I knew now, beyond all reasonable doubt, that I am the worst food shopper in the known civilized world. Maybe even in the furthest reaches of the farthest jungle.

You know how men hate to do this, but I actually called home. There were things called pay phones. I didn't need one. The store wanted me out of there so badly they let me use the store phone.

"Honey, I'm sorry to take so long, but the store doesn't have a baked bean casserole. They don't have French toast either. They have French bread, but not toast."

"What? Let me talk to the cashier!"

So I gave the phone to the cashier. And they both started laughing so hard I thought the poor woman was going to faint. She literally bent over, gasping for breath. All the clerks who had been "helping" me came over. They whispered. And THEY all started laughing.

I stood there like a Methodist at a Mosque (not knowing what to do or what to say).

I could even hear Diane laughing at the other end of the phone, which was lying there on the counter.

I picked up the phone. "C'mon, honey. What's going on?"

Diane tried to talk. It took a while.

"You're looking at the menu! The things I need you to buy are on the other side!"

"Oh," I said, ever eloquent.

The staff spread out and got everything on the actual list. I was out of there in five minutes.

Over the years, I've gotten better at shopping. But not much.

CHAPTER 22

One Broken Nose, Two Resets

Usually, we had a great time up north at grandpa's cottage. Not this time.

Grandpa had purchased a nice new winch for the boat trailer. It was some sort of five-to-one doo-dad with a special sort of what-chamacallit that would make it super-easy to pull the boat up onto the trailer. He bragged and bragged. He told me all about it. How easy it was. How strong it was. How much it made things so much better.

The only thing he didn't tell me was how to use it. I found out—the hard way.

Our family went up for the weekend. It was early in the morning. As usual, I was up at sunrise, ready to go out and not catch fish. I backed the boat trailer into the lake and preceded, for half an hour to try to figure out how to release the winch. There might have been more intricate puzzles developed in ancient Egypt, but I wasn't familiar with those either.

This is probably one of the many reasons why I don't like those multi-colored little cubes where you try to get all the colored cubes to match. Impossible isn't as much fun as you might think.

Finally, I closely inspected the winch and found something that might work. That something was the release for the winch which—at a glorious, five-to-one rate of speed—fractured my nose like never

LOOK BACK AND LAUGH!

before. Mind you, I've broken my nose many times. They used to call me "The Nose" in high school! But this one was a beaut.

Diana woke up to me coughing up blood and spewing it into the bathroom sink. The typical wife, she kept asking, "How did you do this? Why did you do this? What happened?" Men love questions like that. Even if I could have talked, no explanation would have sufficed.

Well, I *tried* to talk. She might as well have been asking me to explain quantum physics. Eventually, I explained that the winch had attacked me.

We got in the car—with all four kids and plenty of paper towels—and sped off to the nearby clinic. Where nobody was except the receptionist. After a few hours, a doctor stopped by and let me know that they really couldn't help me with such a badly fractured nose. My nose wasn't just broken. It was wandering. The doc recommended we take care of it when we got back home.

Believe it or not, we still had a pretty nice time. It takes a lot to discourage us. Since I had so much experience with broken noses, things went pretty well. The kids looked at me a little differently since my nose, both my eyes and a lot of my forehead were turning black and blue.

When we got home, I made an appointment right away to see a nose specialist downtown. He was a kindly little man. He took an X-ray and saw immediately how to fix the nose. Mercifully, he didn't tell me too much about the procedure.

He just sat me down in a reclining chair then told me to close my eyes and relax. I did. Apparently, he had watched too many *Three Stooges* movies. Because he gently took hold at the bottom of my nose with two of his fingers and whispered, "This may hurt a little." He was right.

He then suddenly jerked my nose into the correct position. My entire life passed before my eyes. Even back then, that took a lot of time! I'd been around for quite a while. I've enjoyed counting innumerable stars. Really, I thought to myself, *Now I know. There are a lot of stars!"*

I sat in his lobby for an hour, trying to recover and thinking about eternity. A little later, he explained, "We're going to have to protect your nose so we don't have to do this again." I couldn't have agreed more! "Let's *not* do this again!" I said.

But he put on the most uncomfortable metal piece ever, over my nose with a strap around the back of my head. When I put on my glasses, they were so tilted that any relationship between what I saw and reality was purely coincidental.

When I got home, I vowed to wear the brace as much as possible to protect myself. And I did. Except in bed. I don't wear my glasses in bed. So why would I wear a nose brace in bed?

The next morning—Saturday—I found out why. Our two-year-old son Jeff was standing between us with both hands on the bed board, rocking back and forth while singing a song. Unfortunately, he lost his grip and sat down. He laughed and laughed. And banged his head. Right on to my nose. The pain was incredible, although shockingly familiar.

Actually, the pain wasn't the worst part. It was the anticipation. I knew I was going to have to go see the kindly little doctor again. I knew what the kindly little doctor was going to do to me again. I knew what it was going to feel like again. I really didn't want to go. But I did. And it did.

I never did finish counting all those stars. But I got a really good start on the project. I was up to about 3.2 billion. After that, for two weeks, I even wore the brace in the shower!

Although it was tempting, I didn't change our son's name to "Winch."

CHAPTER 23

Business Trips to Disaster

In my line of work, we had annual business conventions in winter. All of which had the worst luck of anything I've ever experienced. If they hadn't had bad luck, they wouldn't have had any luck at all.

Something always happened. Always.

Every year, Diane and I kept going. But for the life of me, I can't figure out why.

One year, we went to Florida. It was fifty degrees. We tried laying out on the beach. It wasn't the same. Frostbite isn't the same as a sun tan.

Another year, we went to New Orleans for Mardi Gras. But the police went out on strike and the whole thing was canceled. It was so cold that I don't think there would have been much going on anyway. However, Lent came off right on schedule.

When we went to San Antonio, the convention itself came off without a hitch. But they served a Mexican buffet the night before to welcome everyone. The food never said "good-bye" to Diane. She was sick the entire week. Never left the room. I don't think she even left the bathroom.

I literally bought all of the stomach stuff they had at the hotel store. Then I went outside and bought industrial-strength, large bottles of the stuff.

Luckily, Diane recovered by week's end or it would have been a particularly messy plane ride home.

The killer, though, was when the convention booked a week in Las Vegas.

The hotel burned. The hotel actually burned.

We were in the restaurant having dinner at the time. The staff was fantastic. They got everyone out in an orderly fashion. Everyone stayed calm. The gaming tables were all locked down. When we got out, we could see it was a serious fire.

Diane phoned home to let everyone know we were all right. Then I noticed the fire/rescue people had set up a big temporary headquarters nearby. The whole city fire department had rolled out. I asked if I could help as a volunteer.

"Can you type?" a man asked.

"Sure," I said. "Sixty words a minute, no errors."

"Great. Sit here at this desk. Interview each person who got out. Get their names and room numbers. Ask if everyone in the room got out. We'll give that information to the firemen so they know they don't have to go to that room."

I got busy and was glad to do it. They were already carrying out fire fighters who were suffering from smoke inhalation. Those guys are brave beyond all measure. They were literally willing to die to get people out of that hotel.

So. Guests started talking. And I started typing.

Every couple of minutes, a fire official would come by, rip out the paper, and run over to a dispatch radio with the room numbers.

Meanwhile, I was getting quite an education. No one, apparently, was supposed to actually be in Las Vegas. No one was with the people they were actually supposed to be with. It was enlightening, to say the least.

"I'm here, but my wife doesn't know it."

"Name and room number, please. Is everybody out?"

"I'm okay, but I didn't use my real name when I checked in."

"Name [the one you checked in with] and room number, please. Is everybody out?"

"I'm here with my girlfriend. My wife will kill me."

"Name and room number, please. Is everybody out?"

It went on and on like that. The Asian people were the most fun, and there were a lot of them. Most of them had names like the sound of silverware hitting the floor.

"Name and room number please. Can I buy a vowel? Is everybody out?"

I managed to get them to spell it out for me.

After a while, one of the hotel managers wandered by my desk to listen. He was impressed with my typing, but sure had problems with something else.

I heard him talking with the staff. "Who is this guy? He's learning all about our customers!"

So. To make a short story a little shorter, they thanked me profusely and ushered me out. Quickly.

I didn't mind. My fingers were getting sore and, besides, I had done my bit to save mankind (and womankind).

What happens in Vegas stays in Vegas. Almost always.

CHAPTER 24

The Unsightly Nightie

Diane met Allison at church. There was a problem at Allison's house and she needed a little help. They became friends. Practically sisters, really.

One time, they went food shopping together with all the kids. Allison's car was out of commission. They pulled up to the store in our van with all four of our kids and Allison's three. Allison went first and did all of her shopping. All seven kids stayed with Diane in the car. It was mayhem, but Diane handles those situations really well. After all, she's married to me.

Allison came back with her groceries and piled them into the back. Then it was Diane's turn. Naturally, all seven kids wanted to go with her! Realizing that not only was that unfair, it might also end what could be a very nice friendship, Allison decided to come along.

As they were all getting out of the car, Diane noticed that Allison's daughter Rachel was wearing something strange. An old ragged, ripped, faded negligee! Allison hadn't noticed it, but now she was six miles on the other side of appalled.

She asked Rachel, "Honey, why are you wearing that!?"

Rachel was so happy. "I wore it to school for show and tell!"

CHAPTER 25

Our Most Expensive
Free Car Ever

Life has highs and lows. It also has a lot of expensives and cheaps.

During one particular economic low time for us, Diane's brother Bob did something wonderful. He gave us his business car. It had a lot of miles on it but it looked great. Most of the miles were easy, highway miles. It was to be a great sedan for our growing family.

We sure needed the car. We were so grateful.

And happy. Until a week later when the engine went bad. Now we were stuck with a nice looking piece of metal sitting—immobile—in our driveway. Of course, we couldn't tell Bob who had been so nice.

Luckily, we have a friend who does auto body work. He offered to buy a new engine and install it for us. He's a great guy. The price was right. So we went ahead.

Unfortunately, his son bought the engine. "Reconditioned." For cash. From a person, not a store. With no receipt.

Our friend installed it, not knowing what his son had done. We found out as soon as we started the car. The car burned oil like the oil fields in Iraq after the first Gulf War.

He did everything he could to fix the engine. He worked like crazy. So did the engine... crazy.

But because of all our trouble, he did us a favor. Being a body man, he and his son put racing stripes on both sides! That was a nice gesture, but it didn't help. It didn't make the car go any faster either.

We still had a nice looking heap of metal sitting in our driveway. Racing stripes didn't do much. For it or us.

About that time, our oldest daughter Gayle had just learned to drive. She took our other car to the store. Everything was fine until she got home. She didn't turn it back into the driveway correctly. Her turn was too severe. She clipped the side of our "race car."

Now normally, when that happens, a driver will simply back up, readjust, and pull right in. Gayle, being new to this driving business, kept going—slowly, steadily—right across the entire side of our racing car. Leaving a huge, long, deep indentation. All along the side panels, right up to the front wheel.

Just below the racing stripe.

Being a normal teenager, she came into the house and mentioned it. "Dad, I put a little dent in Uncle Bob's car."

"Okay, honey," I said. What did it matter? The darn thing hardly ran anyway. "I'll take a look at it." She ran upstairs. Then I found out why she did that.

I took a look at it. I gasped. I cried. Then I disappeared.

After a while, Diane asked the kids where I was. Jeff took off on his bike, searching for me. It took a while. Eventually, he came back and told her, "Dad is sitting at the end of the street by the creek, throwing pebbles in the water…"

I calmed down. I gave Gayle a few more driving lessons. Now we didn't even have a *good-looking* car that didn't run. Even the racing strip was wrecked. Our driveway looked more like a junk yard than the Indianapolis Speedway after the pile-up.

We traded in the race car at a dealership with a full disclaimer about the engine. We bought another used car. It didn't have a racing stripe but it sure lasted longer.

Free ain't as cheap as you might think.

CHAPTER 26

A Different Dianne and Some Very Different Coffee

We like to get together with other couples.

Usually, things go well. One reason is because my wife is very gracious, considerate, courteous, and careful not to offend others. Like I said, opposites attract.

Our friends Ken and Dianne invited us over for lunch after church. Sounded great to me. But there was a problem. Diane (my Diane... one "n"), said Ken's wife was super-critical about her cooking.

Diane said, "Dianne [that's Dianne... two *N*s'] is so nervous about us coming. She doesn't think she's a good cook. So please be good. Don't you dare complain about the food. Whatever she puts out, you eat it!"

I think there's a Bible verse about that. Anyway, I said, "Sure, I can eat just about anything. No problem."

Off we went to their house. Dianne had fed her kids beforehand. So it was just the four of us for a nice lunch. Things went well. The food was fine. Then she said these now-unforgettable words to me, "Ken and I like coffee, would you like some?"

"Please!" I said. I put in my usual teaspoon of sugar and drank a little.

My mouth exploded.

The two of them were sitting right across from me, happily drinking the coffee. My mouth felt like Vietnam during the war. My face showed it. But I couldn't say anything. My mouth was full of… something.

Now both Diane and Dianne were flustered. Dianne (two *N*s) was so embarrassed. The other Diane (only one *N*) was blowing a gasket.

To this day, I can't believe I actually did what I did. I quickly got up and spit out the coffee into the kitchen sink. Then I grabbed a cup of water to swish around in my mouth. That went into the sink too.

I turned around and there were Ken and Dianne aghast, sitting there with their half-empty cups.

Realizing the lunch (and my marriage) had probably ended, we made a little small talk and then left. Needless, to say, we didn't use the car air conditioning on the way home. It was that cold.

It didn't get any better at home. "How could you do that to her? She's so hurt. I'm so embarrassed. Didn't you see them drinking the same coffee? Didn't I tell you to eat—OR DRINK!—whatever she served?"

Frankly, I didn't remember the drinking part but I knew the proper thing to say. The ancient mantra of all successful husbands.

"I'm sorry, dear."

It's usually effective in all languages all around the world. It's effective in all cultures and most situations. Not this time. It wasn't enough. Our house was enveloped by a polar vortex. (By the way, I never heard the term "polar vortex" until recently. We used to call it "winter.")

But life goes on. Diane let me survive the night. Next morning, it was time for me to drive to work.

When the phone rang.

It was Dianne (two *N*s). She was laughing. Actually, laughing.

Here was the story. Her daughter had come down for breakfast. She always eats cereal and had put a spoonful of sugar on it. Then, just like me, she just about gagged and spit it out into the sink. Then her brother confessed.

He had filled the sugar bowl with salt…

I was never so glad to hear anything in my life. The only reason Ken and Dianne survived was because they drank their coffee black. Diane and I and Dianne laughed so hard our sides hurt.

God has a sense of humor. He must. Because He sure enjoys putting us in crazy situations!

The only thing normal in our house is the setting on the dryer.

CHAPTER 27

Moms, Dads, and the F-Word

I'm not too sharp about anything when it comes to sex. I'm also not especially sharp when it comes to talking about it.

But I got trapped one day.

Our youngest daughter came home from school and used the F-word in front of Mom. That did it. Off to her bedroom they went. My wife was furious.

"You can't talk like that!"

"Girls don't use words like that!" (Remember, dear reader, this was quite a few years ago.)

Our little daughter's defense was simple and direct. "All the kids at school say it. And, Mom, I don't even know what it means. What does it mean anyway?"

What makes mothers say, "You better talk to your dad" when kids say things like that? Desperation? Fright? Revenge?

Who knows? Anyway, that's what Diane said.

Now I had to explain a sexual obscenity to a first-grader.

I thought about it a lot. These days, all I would have had to do was turn on a television sitcom and let her watch it. She would have learned everything. But we Americans were so deprived back them. Family television shows were actually for families.

I was thinking quick. And I actually came up with an answer.

"Honey, you know that Mommy and Daddy love each other, don't you?" Her eyes were wide. "Yes, Daddy."

"Well, moms and dads get together and sometimes a baby is born. We love the baby. That's why we love you and your brothers and sister so much."

Now I had her attention. "Yes, Daddy."

"Well, dogs have puppies. Cats have kittens. Rabbits have bunnies. Do you think they love each other like we love you?"

"No, Daddy."

"Well, honey," I said, hugging her. "That word is about what animals do when they don't love each other. They just do it. And that's what it's called."

"So when you talk about somebody and use that word, you're really calling them an animal."

Her eyes filled with tears. "Really, Daddy? Really?"

She wasn't the only one crying. Diane was listening in the hallway, smiling through the wetness, giving me a big thumb's up.

Our daughter said, "Daddy, I'll never call anybody that ever again."

And she never did.

CHAPTER 28

Horsing around in Sunday School

It was an interesting adult Sunday school class. A woman was teaching us about horses in the Bible. I don't remember too much about the theology involved, but it was interesting.

How Jesus will come to conquer earth at the second coming, with a whole heavenly army following him riding on white horses. (Which convinces me, by the way, that there are animals in heaven.)

How Psalms talks about war horses. How the Chaldeans had stallions. How the Egyptians had chariots drawn by horses. How horse-drawn chariots could drive three abreast around the top of the walls at Nineveh.

Then she started talking about a famous jockey who was a devout Christian. He was outspoken about his strong faith and how it had helped all through his professional horse-racing career. In fact, she said, he had written about it in a wonderful book.

But she couldn't remember the title of the book.

"I just can't remember it," she said. "You should all read it. My goodness, it's right on the tip of my tongue."

I piped up.

"The Sermon on the Mount?"

CHAPTER 29

Little Mr. Manners

"Mom likes the other kids better than me."

Little five-year-old Jeff looked at me with all the wide-eyed earnestness he could muster. I tried to reason with him, but nothing seemed to register.

"We love all you kids the same! We have no favorites! Mom and Dad just add more love every time a new baby shows up."

But he wasn't convinced. I could see it in his eyes and his slumping shoulders.

I thought fast. And for once, my brainstorm actually worked. Lightning struck.

I sat down with him, put my arm around his shoulders and said, "Listen, Jeff, here's what you do. The next time we're all walking up to the house, you run up there first and hold open the door for Mom. I promise you she'll notice and love you to death! Got it?"

He looked doubtful. "That's all? That'll work?"

"Don't worry," I said. "Moms appreciate things like that. They don't like doors anyway! Now don't say anything to anyone. Just do it, okay?"

"Sure, Dad," he said with all the enthusiasm he showed when eating peas.

But he didn't tell anyone. Neither did I.

That Sunday, we came home from church. I purposely didn't pull into the garage. (It was on purpose because, as usual, there was no room in the garage for a car!)

We were walking up to the door. But apparently, Jeff had forgotten all about our deal. I looked back at him and caught his attention. I grimaced at him and nodded toward. He remembered!

He raced up to the door and held it open for Diane, beaming like he'd just won the lottery. Diane reacted like she *had* won the lottery! "Oh, Jeff! How nice! What a fine little gentleman you are!"

If Jeff had smiled any bigger, his ears would have bent.

From then on, it never stopped. Every door was opened. Every time he could, he was courteous to his mother. This, of course, did not extend to his sisters. But, hey, I promised you the reader that everything in this book is true.

Jeff even got a job at the local grocery store and volunteered to take out bags of groceries for the ladies. Putting the food into the car and then even opening the car door for them if they wished. The store kept smelling salts on hand for fainting spells.

The ending of this story is even happier than the middle.

Jeff went off to college in Texas, just like his big brother. He noticed a nice, young Lone Star State girl at church one day. He got up his nerve and asked her out.

When she got home from their first date, she told her mother, "Mom, I'm going to marry him!"

"What? After one date?"

"Oh, Mom! He held the car door open for me. He adjusted my seat at the restaurant when we sat down. He was so courteous! He was wonderful!"

"I'm going to marry him… !"

And she did!

The nice guy (and a wonderful girl) finished first!

CHAPTER 30

When Mom Met the Mouse

Our dog Piper was the best. Loved us all a ton. Never gave us any problems.

The only complication was that somewhere in her galaxy of genes there must have been a hunter. No bird was allowed to fly over our yard undetected or unwarned. No rabbits, no squirrels, no snakes. No nothing.

And especially, no mice.

One evening, Piper wanted to go down into the basement. She just kept sitting by the door, wagging her tail, sniffing at the bottom of the door. There was not a whole lot down there. My tool bench, the freezer, the washer, and the dryer.

But Piper was persistent. I opened the door. And, much to my amazement, she stayed down there all night.

Next morning, we all got up. Piper came up from the basement and I let her out. The kids and I were watching TV in the family room. Diane went downstairs to do a little laundry.

Then she yelled, "John! Piper pooped in the basement. I just stepped in it!"

I sprang into action (after I stopped laughing). "Really?" I asked. "Piper never does that!"

Then came the bloodcurling scream. Diane came up the stairs like Secretariat coming from the back of the pack. Like Mario

Andretti driving on the final lap. Like a football wide receiver on a post pattern.

Like… well, you get the picture. She was coming fast.

She was also screaming, waving both arms up in the air. It wasn't dog poop she had stepped in.

It was a mouse. Or what remained of one.

A mouse that Piper had caught and chewed on for a while.

After several seconds of additional hysteria, I had Diane sit down and I cleaned the various mouse parts off the bottom of her foot. (And from in between her toes.)

By now, all four kids were gathered around, wide-eyed. They all wanted to see the mouse. Or what was left of it. The girls thought it so gross. The boys thought it was so cool. Diane thought it was the end of the world as we know it.

I don't think Diane ever forgave Piper.

I don't know why women and elephants have so much trouble with mice. Both never forget.

I know Diane will never forget that mouse.

The kids didn't either. For years—and I mean for years—all they needed to do to have a laugh was ask, "Remember the time Mom stepped on a mouse?"

How could any of us forget?

We would all laugh. Except Diane.

Not Diane.

CHAPTER 31

The Time We Burned Out as Marriage Counselors

It was an interesting call from the church.

Our pastor was counseling a couple who wanted to get married. It would be the second marriage for both of them. He thought it would be great if they could have dinner with a happily married couple, just to see what a good marriage looks like.

So he called us. He actually called us.

But we were happy to have dinner with them. So was the couple.

It seemed to be a nice compliment being asked to do this. Diane was busy preparing a nice meal. The eager couple showed up early. Luckily, we had the house picked up. We had farmed out the kids. It was all good.

We visited with them out in the driveway. For quite a while. Our dog had had puppies and they were corralled in the garage. Of course, we had to visit with them.

Every time I see puppies, I think of the famous quote from John L. Sullivan, the old-time boxer. "I can lick any man in the house!"

Then we came *into* the house and noticed a slight problem.

The kitchen was in flames.

Diane had been frying some green peppers, which apparently are flammable. Not always, but this time for sure. I put the fire out, breaking every rule in the firefighting book. You don't throw water onto a grease fire. It works eventually. Just don't stand too close or be surprised by the splatter.

Anyway, we were in trouble. The house was a mess. Oily smoke everywhere. I was amazed at how much damage had been done to that entire level of the house.

Later, when we had a chance to think about it, we realized we should have just locked up the house and gone out some place for dinner.

Of course, we didn't. We decided to clean up the place.

It wasn't easy. Greasy smoke didn't seem to want to come off. We took down curtains. Tried to clean walls. The smeared "Early American Depression" look was unique and eclectic.

Also, it was startling to realize how many cobwebs we had missed (or never noticed) on the ceiling. They, too, were all black with grease. All the black little spiders blended right in.

After a few hours of hard work and very interesting conversation, we actually sat down in all that mess to eat some sort of supper.

We laughed about it all. All four of us. We actually laughed about it.

They were smiling when they left. They got married.

Unfortunately, their marriage didn't last.

Ours did.

Somehow.

But the church never called again to recommend us…

CHAPTER 32

The Night Mom Got Shot

It all started with our "new" waterbed. Actually, it wasn't new. It was old. But it was new to us.

Unlike newer models, the mattress had no internal separators. Thus, it was never level. It made waves like those big machines at water parks. When I got in, Diane's entire body would rise about a foot.

Needless to say, it didn't do much for our love life. If either one of us was in the mood, I'd start swimming over there. By the time we actually got together, I had either forgotten why I was going or was too tired to function.

Our only other option was to both collapse to the center. But then neither of us could move. It was a whole new dimension of platonic intimacy.

We bought the darn thing because people said we'd be able to sleep better. But sleep was another problem. We couldn't get any.

The heater wasn't too good. We both tossed and turned. Or, you could say, *we* because it was cold, we always woke up sore.

Another problem was actually getting out of the bed. It took several minutes. I finally developed a strategy of rolling over the side. It was effective but not easy.

It was kind of like "stop, drop, and roll" if you've caught on fire. Which is also hard to do (catching on fire) when you're in a waterbed.

When I *did* get out, Diane always woke up when her altitude nosedived on her side of the bed. It was the same with me. If we couldn't get together when we were in the water bed, at least we'd both get up together when we got out of the darn thing.

It all came to a head one night when our son Jeff stayed out late. His biological clock had no relation to sunrise, sunset, the stars, the calendar, or digits and dials. It was never what time it was. It was always what time he *felt* it was.

Our other kids were asleep. Diane and I were both trying to imitate them.

All of a sudden, Diane was yelling, "Wake up! Wake up! I've been shot!"

I did my best roll-out-of-a-moving-car imitation to get on solid ground. Still half asleep, I yelled for the kids. "Wake up, everybody! Wake up! Mom's been shot!"

In my mental state—which was semi-comatose—her statement actually sounded intelligent. The fact that we slept on the second floor, lived in the suburbs, had never heard a gunshot (no one could even hunt in our town except with a bow and arrow) and we hadn't even heard a car backfire—none of that seemed to matter.

Doggone it, when your wife has been shot, a husband ought to be able to do something about it!

I staggered around, bumping into everything until we got the light on. I was finally able to stand. Diane floundered, trying to get up. (She hadn't mastered my stop-drop-and-roll technique.) "I can't feel my arm!" she yelled. "My arm! My arm! I've been shot!"

We all bought it hook, line, and sinker.

Our youngest daughter ran downstairs to find bandages. As she ran by the front door, our son Jeff banged on it to get her attention. She did what any normal person would do under the same circumstances. She wet her pants. Life can be cruel. Wet, sometimes, too. But cruel.

We let Jeff in and the whole story came out. He had stayed out late but left his key at home. He knocked and knocked at the front door, but we were asleep. The doorbell didn't work (an ongoing constant all throughout our marriage regardless of where we lived).

Desperate, he decided to throw pebbles up at our bedroom window. In her sleep, Diane thought the noise was a gunshot. Meanwhile, lying on her side in our wretched waterbed, her left arm had gone to sleep.

So "naturally"—or not so naturally (we use that term advisedly in our house)—she thought she'd been shot in the arm.

All ended well. Our daughter put the bandages away. Our son—properly admonished—went to bed. As usual, it was my job to clean up the mess. Diane thoroughly checked her body for any new orifices. Finding none, she was actually able to go back to sleep. Her arm and everything.

For some reason, I had a little more difficulty.

CHAPTER 33

Parent's Night in When the Kids Went Out

Our son Karl finally got his car license. Like all sixteen-year-olds who get their license, he was ready to go! Anywhere! Any time! Give a ride to anybody!

Diane and I were not so surprised but very delighted when he offered to take our three other kids to a movie. We had a little parental trepidation but we finally agreed.

Besides, I looked it Diane with that special look and raised my eyebrows a little. A romantic night alone sounded like a good idea. Extremely unusual, but potentially very nice.

We curled up on the couch and watched a very romantic news broadcast together.

It was a lovely show—something about crime, politics, and bad weather. The reruns are still on. We would've kept watching for a while, but romance was beckoning. That's when we heard the car pull into the driveway and the kids run up to the door, laughing.

They piled in with a pizza and two big bottles of soda. "We decided to come home!" they said. "We thought you might be lonely!"

We hadn't been. But we pretended.

Love isn't always sexy. But loving your children is always wonderful.

Besides, eventually they all fall asleep.

That night when I said my prayers, I thanked God they hadn't come home a little later.

CHAPTER 34

The Politest Fire Alarm Ever

"I need to clean the oven," Diane said.

"Okay," I said, "I need to get the car fixed."

"Well," she said, "it's a self-cleaning oven, so I'll just set it and go. And you can go get the car fixed. Karl is old enough to watch the kids."

Since our car is not self-repairing—and the oven *was* self-cleaning—that sounded like a plan.

She left. So did I. I drove the car to the service station which was a few blocks away and started to walk back.

What could go wrong?

What *did* go wrong was the self-cleaning oven belching smoke into our house. Poor Karl thought the place was burning down and got everyone out. But now what? The little guy ran across the street to Shirley's house.

Note: Shirley was a nurse who worked nights. Karl knew that much. He hated to ring the doorbell at nine in the morning. But he did. Several times.

When poor, bleary-eyed Shirley answered the door, she asked, "Oh, Karl, what do you want?"

"Good morning. I'm so sorry. Did I wake you up?"

"It's okay, Karl."

"I know you work at night. You need to sleep."

"It's fine, Karl. What can I do for you?"

"Our house is on fire."

"WHAT!"

I was walking home from the service station when I heard the whole volunteer fire department rolling down the street, sirens blaring, lights flashing. I looked just ahead as they all turned onto our street! "A house might be on fire on our block!" I thought. "I'd better run."

So I did, just as firemen were coming into our front door. "It's in the kitchen," I yelled. "It's an electric stove. I'll switch off the power downstairs!"

"Thanks!" they said, running upstairs.

The place wasn't on fire, but it was filled with smoke. They set up big fans to get most of it out. It was a mess, but the guys were great. Diane drove up just as the trucks were leaving.

One of the guys stepped over to me. "Thanks a lot for helping us there."

"I kind of *had* to. It's my house!"

He smiled. "Yes, I guess you did!"

That's when Shirley came over. I guess a couple hours of sleep would have to be enough. There was no way she was going to be able to sleep after a morning like this.

"You have the politest son ever," she said, hugging him.

Calm, too.

CHAPTER 35

Grandpa's Propeller

As was usually the case, Diane and I were flat broke. There's something about kids and money. The kids stay. The money goes.

As was also usually the case, we decided to spend our last few dollars on something completely unnecessary… but fun.

A weekend in Northern Wisconsin at her parents' cabin seemed like a great idea. We packed everybody and everything.

We'll arrived late at night and went right to sleep. First thing next morning (sunrise), I got up early to go out fishing in their boat. Naturally, I didn't catch anything. I didn't mind really because not catching fish is a longstanding family tradition. When we go on vacation, the fish go on vacation too.

That's why they call it "fishing," not "catching."

One thing bothered me. The boat didn't seem to have much power. When I got back to the dock, I raised the motor. The propeller was ruined. The lake was low and I had bottomed out.

Now what? No propeller. No money. And no way to use the boat—for us now or for grandpa later. There was only one thing to do: buy another propeller. And we needed to do it this weekend, using the very last margin we had on our last credit card. I put the new propeller on the motor. We didn't touch the boat for the rest of the weekend.

That made for a dull getaway… but a safe and less potentially expensive time.

Besides, there were a lot of fish under the dock. Little fish to be sure. But our kids were little, too. Our weekend ended well.

A few weeks later, my father in law went up to the cottage. Naturally, I wanted to know how things were going. When I called, he said, "Wow, I didn't know the lake was so low! I bottomed out on the way in and ruined the propeller. So I decided to buy a new, Teflon propeller. It's super strong! We won't have any trouble from now on!"

What a tremendous sense of regret, relief, frustration, and bankruptcy spread over me!

But I learned my lesson.

Even failure ain't cheap!

CHAPTER 36

Dog's Life Isn't So Bad

All through our marriage, Diane and I have owned dogs. Most wonderful, a few not. A few years ago, I saw a wonderful video. It's called "God and Dog" by Wendy Francisco. You can find it on the internet. Just go to www.youtube.com and type in "God and dog." The lyrics are terrific.

> I look up and I see God.
> I look down and see my dog.
> Simple spelling—G-O-D.
> Same word backwards—D-O-G.
> They would stay with me all day.
> I'm the one who walks away.
> But both of them just wait for me.
> And dance at my return with glee.
> Both love me no matter what.
> Divine God. Canine Mutt.
> I've seen love from both sides now.
> It's everywhere. Amen. Bow wow.
> (Copyright 2009, Wendy Francisco)

It got me to thinking about dogs.

Our son Jeff is convinced that, thousands of years ago, dogs got together and had a bright idea. "Look, we've got two choices. We can either stay out here in the cold and eat or be eaten… or we can go live with the humans. What do you think?"

So they checked it out. When the report came back, it was almost too good to be true. "It'll be great! They'll feed us, give us water, keep us warm, pet us, let us lay around the house, offer free obstetrics care and give us exercise."

"They'll even walk behind us, pick up what we leave behind and put it in bags! All we have to do is act happy when they show up and act sad when they leave! I'm not kidding!"

"What do you think?"

Who would pass up a deal like that?

Personally, I'm a big fan of dogs. Who else would give you a polka-dot lawn in the summer, free excavation service in your yard, rounded edges on your wood furniture at no charge, free paw print patterns on your kitchen floor whenever it rains, a portable pillow for your kids, a loud burglar alarm for anything that looks, sounds or smells like a burglar (and that covers an awful lot of stuff!), free greeter service at the door, free junk mail prevention (in fact, prevention of *all* mail deliveries if you're not careful). The benefits are endless.

Then, of course, there's the friendliness. Not like cats.

- Dogs come when you call. Cats take a message.
- Dogs chase a stick when you throw it. Cats look at you like you're nuts.
- You can't get eight cats to pull a sled through snow.
- Dogs believe they're human. Cats believe they're God.
- Dogs care. Cats stare.

As a pastor, I knew you could wash a dog. But you can't baptize a cat.

What's the bottom line?

Cats do what they want. They're totally unpredictable. They constantly work on their hair. When you want to play, they want to be alone. When you want to be alone, they want to play. Maybe that's why so many women like cats…

On the other hand, dogs lay around in the most comfortable chair. They can hear a package of food opening half a block away. When you want to play, they want to play. When you want to be alone, they want to play. Maybe that's why so many men like dogs. I'm just sayin'.

The most fun I ever had was with our Golden Doodle Izzy. She loved to ride with us in the car. When we'd get out, she'd stay in but would always sit in the driver's seat until I got back. Cute as the dickens.

Well, it didn't take too long for my imagination to run wild. Whenever we'd be walking back to the car and there were some kids around, I'd say, "Where's my car? It's not where I parked it? What's going on?"

"Oh, there it is!" I'd point to Izzy in the front seat. "Did you move the car again? I told you not to drive it!"

The kids would be wide-eyed. Their mom would be laughing.

But they all understood after I explained.

"Ever since she got that dog license, she thinks she can drive!"

A dog's life ain't bad. The owner's ain't either!

CHAPTER 37

To and from — and to and from — Nashville

Our daughter Gayle was a positive, hardworking, and determined young lady—with the worst luck of any person I've ever met.

One time, she decided to make a new start. So she answered a want ad from a medical group in Nashville, Tennessee. She was hired immediately, which meant it was time to move her everything from Milwaukee down south. With no money, of course. Parents exist for times like this.

Our son Karl and I piled all her stuff onto a rented trailer, hooked it up to our old van and took off for her new apartment in Nashville. Gayle drove ahead in her car. We followed way behind in our van.

Frankly, I was amazed that our daughter had accumulated so many things. There was a lot!

Actually, there was a *tremendous* amount of stuff. More importantly, there was a tremendous amount of *heavy* stuff. So heavy, in fact, that it destroyed the transmission of our old van.

We ended up pretty much dead on the road, somewhere in Tennessee. Not near Nashville. Just somewhere.

Believe it or not, we managed to pull off the road into an old junk yard. We met the owner who had pity on us. I still can't believe it, but he actually let us take one of his old trucks, hook up our trailer, and continue to Nashville. What a nice guy!

The deal was that we would pick up a rental car in Nashville and, after we were done unloading the trailer, leave the rental trailer in Nashville and drive the truck and rented car back to his place. That's what we did.

And that *is* what we did, eventually. Unfortunately, the borrowed truck wasn't quite up to it. It thought Nashville was farther away than we did.

It broke down three times. Each time, the man's son would come out and get it running again. Slowly but surely, and in anything but a timely fashion, we made it to Nashville. We unloaded the trailer, turned it in at the rental place, kissed Gayle goodbye, got a rental car, and headed off for Milwaukee.

Of course, we had to return the truck. Which we did. At eleven o'clock at night.

We were getting our personal stuff out of the old van. Who would think that a county deputy would be cruising along a rural road, checking out the local auto junk yards?

But we should've thunk it. Because there he was. He had seen our flashlight as we went through the van.

"How ya'll doing?"

(For those of you who may not be familiar with the Southern regions of the United States, "How ya'll doing?" is drawl for "You have the right to remain silent. You have the right to an attorney. Anything you say can be held against you in a court of law, etc.")

"Hi, Officer. My son and I were moving my daughter to Nashville. Our van broke down. This nice man let us take his truck…"

"He *let* you take his truck… ?"

"Well, yes. He loaned it to us. I made a deal that he could keep our van. I don't have the title because I already signed it over to him. We just got our personal stuff out of the van and took off the Wisconsin plates. His truck is over there. The keys are in it with a thank you note on the front seat. We filled up the gas tank and left it here."

The nice deputy looked at me.

I'm sure he was thinking the same thing I was thinking. "WHO IN THE WORLD would make up a story like that?"

He let us go. Even years later, Karl still says it would have topped it all off if he had arrested us. We'd have spent the night in jail. But I suppose that would have been cheaper than a motel. Safer, too. Maybe.

Anyway, we drove the rental car back to Milwaukee.

What an adventure. We were sure glad it was over, though.

Gayle was happy. She had a new life. I wasn't so thrilled. I needed a new car.

Parents exist for times like this.

Everything was fine until we got a call two days later. It was Gayle. "I got fired!" she cried. "I want to come home!"

My wife and I looked at each other. My son and I looked at each other. I must admit that I had quite a few funny thoughts about leaving her in Nashville (emphasize "funny"—I was joking… probably).

My wife—always practical—had a good thought. Go down there and bring her back. Karl needed to get back to college in Texas. We could take his car to Nashville.

We'd rent a big truck there. Karl would help pack it up, then go on to Texas. I would get all of Gayle's stuff into the big box truck. She could drive back in her car.

In situations like that, I've learned that my wife's opinion becomes our opinion immediately. And real fast. Or it better.

Like the sign says on my desk: "The opinions of the husband are not necessarily those of the management."

So with no money but, fortunately, with a little bit of fudge left on our credit card, Karl and I took off again for Nashville. At least we didn't need a map. We knew the way.

As we were going down, we drove past the auto junkyard in Tennessee. I glanced wistfully at our old van.

We rented a big box truck in Nashville. Karl and I packed up Gayle's stuff. A one-way trip rental was way more expensive. Then my son drove on to college. I brought back the truck full of Gayle's stuff—with her driving behind, crying—all the way back to Milwaukee. She sobbed all the way, weaving through the tears.

94

Then when we got back, she immediately found a new job where she was much happier and made more money.

She didn't even have to learn how to drawl.

Oh well. Parents exist for times like this.

CHAPTER 38

Yet Another Nightgown Story

Parents always know.

I discovered this very early in life. Whenever I tried to get away with anything or shade the truth, Mom and Dad always found out.

However, now as a parent, I realize how it's done. And *why* it happens. You see, parents have tried to pull off so much naughty stuff in their lives that they're on to everything. They know what to look for. Their poor kid doesn't have a chance!

Our son Karl didn't understand that. Even as a teenager.

One weekend, Diane and I left to visit some friends overnight. Karl was old enough to be in charge. But we told him firmly, "No parties when we're not here!"

The weekend went well… for Diane and I. We got back and were instantly suspicious. You would have been, too, if you were us. (Wow, now that I think about it, you probably *wouldn't* want to be us! But I digress.).

The problem was simple. The house was too clean.

Our house was never "too clean." It wasn't messy. Occasionally, someone *did* put something away. Not too often, but sometimes.

We were instantly suspicious. Completely suspicious. Totally suspicious.

But we had nothing to go on.

Until we discovered the negligee under our pillow.

We put it back, of course. Then we called Karl to our bedroom.

"Okay," I said. "You've got one chance and one chance only. You're going to tell us who was here while we were gone. If you tell us anything else but the truth, the whole truth and nothing but the truth, you're really going to get it."

Karl was amazed. "Aw, Dad. I had a party. But I only invited the guys over to play board games. How did you know?"

"Well, son," I said. "The house was awful clean."

I was thinking about those old western movies when the cowboy is looking out for Indians. "It's quiet out there, too quiet."

The house was clean. Too clean.

"You mean I'm in trouble for cleaning up the house too much?"

"No," said Diane. "But you said you only had your friends—boys—for your party. What about this?" She took the negligee out from under the pillow. "If this belongs to one of the guys, that's even worse!"

Karl was flabbergasted.

"I found it in the dirty clothes downstairs. I thought it was yours! So I put it under your pillow!"

It was my turn to talk. But I couldn't. I was laughing too hard. Diane looked daggers at me but my shoulders were shaking. Pretty soon, Diane started to smile, then giggle. Then all three of us were roaring.

It turned out that our daughter Keri had a sleepover the previous weekend. One of her friends had a negligee but it was ripped. Keri said Diane would repair it so she put it down the clothes chute to get it clean.

Karl found it downstairs. Innocently (actually, not so much at the time), he cleaned it and put it under Diane's pillow.

But he forgot one thing.

Mom hasn't worn a negligee since 1968.

CHAPTER 39

Our Romantic
Camping Weekend

Four children are three and a half too many to maintain any type of romantic relationship. If you are newly married and don't know this, you soon will.

Children can become the world's most effective birth control devices.

One summer, Diane decided we needed to get away. The kids were older. We had a camper. For a change, we had a few extra bucks at the end of the month. She made all the plans. Made all the arrangements.

Planned all our meals with a delightful anticipation of eating "adult" food!

Omelets instead scrambled eggs. Steaks instead of hot dogs and hamburgers. Wine coolers. Actual wine coolers! We kept the expenses low so we could finally go out on a couple dates. The weekend finally arrived and off we went.

The first day was wonderful. We lazed around. Ate good—and too much. That night, we decided to go to a stock car race—a first for us. We had a blast and it didn't cost much.

Our getaway was off to a great start.

The next morning, Diane actually agreed to go fishing with me. Astoundingly—amazingly, given our track record—we actually caught fish.

This sky was starting to cloud over but we were having a wonderful time.

When we got back to the campsite, we got ready for lunch. That's when we heard a car horn. It was our two sons and our dog. They let the dog out while pulling up to our camp site. It had been raining for a while and our beloved dog jumped into the camper and right onto our bed. Wet, muddy and happy.

"What's going on?" I asked.

"We thought you would be lonely!" Karl said. "How is it going?"

Words escaped me. Fortunately, my temper escaped me, too.

Naturally, everything changed. Our menu changed (hot dogs and hamburgers). Our budget was busted (the boys wanted to go jet skiing. They jet skied, we paid). Our dog couldn't avoid the mud and neither could the inside of our camper. I will admit, we laughed and laughed. Overall, we had a great time.

Who needs romance anyway? Maybe companionship is better than intimacy.

Maybe.

CHAPTER 40

The Car Always Broke Down at Dairy Queen

Ever since we had kids—and, now, grandkids—our cars have broken down at Dairy Queen.

I'd wait for the right moment. When we were coming up to a Dairy Queen, I'd go into my act. "The car is out of control! I can't do a thing with it! It's got a mind of its own! It's turning! It's turning!"

It always lurched right into the Dairy Queen parking lot. "Oh well," I'd say. "Maybe we should let the car sit here for a while and cool off. Let's eat something!"

It got to the point where the kids were actually rooting for the car to have trouble!

One night, I drove the kids and one of their friends home from the church group. Sure enough, the car went out of control. We ended up right in the Dairy Queen parking lot. We all got out.

I didn't notice their friend was very quiet. She was a lovely little adopted girl from India. "Must be cultural," I thought.

She seemed happy enough with her cone. But, like I said, quiet.

When we all got home, her mother phoned laughing so hard she could hardly talk.

Her daughter had come home breathless. "Mom, the car went out of control! The dad couldn't steer it at all! We ended up at the ice cream store. So we decided to eat something. Then the car cooled off and was okay. Mom, we could have had an accident!"

The mom could barely contain herself. She explained it all to her daughter, then called us laughing. After that, I have to admit I toned it down a little, especially when someone else's kids were in the car.

Things were different quite a few years later when our son Karl went off to college in Texas.

One time, he was driving down there and went through a winter storm in Oklahoma. In that neck of the woods, wet winter storms make the highway an ice rink.

Lots of places down South only use salt for popcorn. Other times, the ice is just too thick. Like right then.

Karl was going slow but, even at that, lost control, did several unplanned donuts and rammed into a concrete divider. He wasn't hurt, but the car was pretty much totaled.

So he hitched a ride to a Dairy Queen (of which there are several million in Oklahoma and Texas).

And what does he say? "Dad, the car went out of control. I'm calling from Dairy Queen."

"Right, Karl," I said, "and what did you order?"

"Oh no, Dad. Really, I had an accident. The car really did break down. In fact, it's wrecked! I called my friends in Dallas. Their dad is going to pick me up and drive me to school."

"Are you okay?" I asked.

"Yes, Dad. I'm really sorry about the car."

"No problem," I said. "If you're okay, I'm okay. By the way, Karl, what are you going to order?"

"Chocolate, Dad."

CHAPTER 41

A Cold Ride to Old New York

I decided to go into full-time Christian ministry after 911.

If those terrorists had attacked us for religious reasons, I decided it was time to get into the spiritual fight. Soon, it was time for Diane and I to move from our beloved Wisconsin to my first pastoral position in Rochester, New York.

It was exciting. We packed all our stuff into a rental truck. Well, actually not. We only *tried* to load up our truck. I mean, all we had was the largest truck we could rent. Unfortunately, there was too much stuff and not nearly enough truck.

Like most people, we had never realized how much God blessed us until we tried to move it all.

One funny thing happened. When we had moved from our previous house, my son and I were packing. We came across an old box with a bunch of junk in it. Like all wives I've ever met, Diane didn't want to throw anything out until she had "a chance to go through it."

There was no time for that. So Karl and I taped it up. We always put a little sign on each box. "What do you want to write on it?" he asked. This is what I wrote. "A box we'll never open and stuff we'll never use."

When we packed up this time to go to Rochester, wouldn't you know we came across that exact same box, packed years ago! With the exact same sign! When we both stopped laughing, we loaded it into the truck.

I didn't have the heart to throw it away…

Anyway, getting back to *this* move.

There certainly wasn't any room for my cherished fishing boat and trailer. Being a true Green Bay Packed fan, I had painted the boat green and the trailer gold. We sold it for cash, all of which was wet from my tears.

There was also no room for our almost antique camper trailer. We sold it for cash, not nearly enough to compensate for all the memories we saw driving away.

Sometimes you have to sell things that are just priceless.

The rest we crammed into the truck. We also had to rent a special trailer for behind the truck. We needed it for our second car, our trusty Ford Taurus.

We were finally ready. Me and our golden retriever Casey were in the cab of the truck, which was hauling our Taurus. Diane was driving behind us in our old beater sedan.

It was going to be a wild but great ride. It wasn't just cold. It was bitter, below zero, bone-chilling cold. See your breath inside the cab of the truck cold.

Things got off to a fairly bad start. Casey loved to drive with us. He was never a problem. So I was little surprised when he threw up all over the front seat. But he seemed relieved to let it all out.

I dutifully cleaned it up. My wife was a nurse. She didn't mind cleaning up a mess from people. She drew the line at dogs.

We gassed up the truck and Diane's car. Then we were on our way. Through cold Chicago. Through colder Indiana. Then through frigid Ohio. Antarctic Pennsylvania was coming soon.

We realized how cold it was when we noticed that everything everywhere was dark. No lights anywhere. At first I thought we were driving through the boonies. But the power was out. All of it. We turned on the car radios only to find out the entire eastern half of Ohio was blacked out.

Cold always seems colder when it's dark.

Unfortunately, the truck and I—and Diane in the other car—were also having a blackout. No gas. We drove past one highway exit after another, looking for lights. Finally, we couldn't wait any longer.

It was either drive to a gas station or coast to a gas station.

In desperation, we pulled into a dark service station. The owner said power was out everywhere. "Maybe you can find a gas station with a generator," he said. *That might be a little tough,* I thought. And maybe dangerous. Both our truck and Diane's car were *below* empty.

But I had an idea! We could take the good old Taurus off the trailer and drive it to find gas!

Diane looked at me a little sheepishly. "Uh, I went shopping in the Taurus before we left," she said. "I knew we wouldn't need any gas in it on the way to New York. So when it was on empty, I didn't get any gas for it!"

"The Taurus is on empty, too?"

Terrific. The temperature was below any thermometer reading ever registered and so were all three of our gas tanks! Our situation was ridiculous.

Even in the midst of all this misery, I had to laugh. Things couldn't get any worse, could they? Events were to prove me wrong.

We decided to take the Taurus with no gas as opposed to the other car and truck with no gas. It got better mileage. Which is tough for any car to do with no gas… but whatever.

Luckily, we *did* find a gas station with a working generator. We filled up the Taurus and drove back for the truck and the other car. A whole posse of desperate drivers figured out that we had found gas.

So Diane and I—after we pulled the Taurus back onto the trailer—led an entire caravan of vehicles to the other gas station.

Eternally grateful, I filled up the tanks and we got back on the road before the long line of thirsty cars behind us drained the gas station completely.

Wow, it was cold. Really cold. Ice on the inside of the windshield—with a defroster on—cold. Iced tea cold—without the tea.

And dark. In a coal mine at midnight dark. The only lights we saw were headlights and tail lights. We hit Pennsylvania and so, naturally, it started to snow. I was amazed that it could still snow when it was so cold. But it can. A lot.

It was getting late. We were dog tired....and not just because we had Casey along with us. It was time to stop.

But where? We still had the same problem. There was no power. Everyplace was blacked out. We finally picked an exit and got off the highway. We came to a town and saw someone walking. I couldn't believe someone would be outside walking on such a cold night. But there he was.

I asked, "Is there a nearby motel?"

"Y-Y-Y-You're in luck!" he said, shivering. "There's a brand-new motel just down the road. They just opened up! I hear it's real nice. There's no traffic on the road so I'm sure you'll get a room."

Sure enough! There it was. I won't mention the name because, even after all these years, the statute of limitations may not have run out. It looked great, though. A brand-new motel.

However, it wasn't shiny. After all, there were no lights. The owners met us in the lobby with candles. We registered in the dark. I felt duty-bound to let them know we had a dog.

"How large is it?" they asked. "Oh, not that big," I answered, crossing my fingers behind my back. Casey *was* small, for a golden retriever. Besides, other than throwing up in the truck (for the first time ever!), he was wonderful dog that had never given us any trouble.

Cross my fingers and hope to die. Really.

Nonetheless, we decided to come in through the side door rather than the lobby. We brought in only our small overnight bag with the essentials. Casey seemed happy enough.

Of course, when we got to the room, my flashlight immediately ran out of batteries. But not before we were able to get unpacked and into bed.

Getting to sleep was no problem. Good. We both needed it.

It was around 2:00 AM when Diane woke me out of the deepest sleep I can ever remember. This wasn't sleep. This was a coma.

I dragged myself into some state of consciousness and she asked, "What is that awful smell?"

It was Casey, throwing up *again*. This time, all over the beautiful new carpeting. It was easy enough to find, but not to see. You guessed it. I had to sniff around for it.

I put an entire roll of toilet paper to good use, extremely glad the toilet was able to flush. I got most of it cleaned up. All that I could feel, that is. (Yuck, those words are even awful to write!) I thought I'd get it nice and really clean in the morning.

But I was really ticked off at Casey. Had he eaten a forty-pound bag of dog food? Digested a rabbit? A bucket of dead dish? How could he be throwing up so much? I dragged him into the bathroom and shut the door.

"Enough is enough!" I whispered. I have to admit it was the first time in our entire marriage I was able to make an angry statement without shouting. Of course, there were other people probably in the next room. But, still, I was actually quiet. Some lessons take a long time to learn.

Back to bed. Another coma. Until four thirty. That's when Diane woke me up out of the second deep sleep. Guess what? Same question! "What is that awful smell?"

I don't have that good of a sniffer, but I knew right away this wasn't going to be fun. Casey hadn't thrown up in the bathroom.

He'd had the biggest case of diarrhea I *never* smelled. I have, however, smelled a skunk. This was worse.

Remember, Diane doesn't do dogs. Remember, still no power. Still no lights.

I dragged the poor dog out the side door and put him in the cab of the truck. It was cold, but I figured he had a lot of hair. Besides, the truck would be safe. The poor dog couldn't have had anything left inside him.

Then it was back to the room, in the dark. In the total dark. I brought in an entire box full of paper towels and started to feel my way around the tile floor in the bathroom, cleaning up the you know what and flushing it down the you know where.

It wasn't easy. It was, on the other hand, everywhere. Usually, Casey had done his business in only on place. Either he did this on the run or he had walked around in it for a while.

I worked for over an hour. In the dark. I smelled as bad as the room. I was hoping it looked better than it smelled. Just then, the lights went back on. With light, I saw just how bad a job I had done.

It was 5:30 AM. The sun would be out soon. Daylight was coming. We not only had to get the room clean again. We had to plan our getaway!

I went back out to the truck and got every cleaning supply I could reach. Every rag and towel I could put my hands on.

You, the dear reader, will be so proud that—even in this, literally after our darkest hour—we decided not to use the motel towels! I had sincere compassion for these poor owners of this brand new motel.

I also have a deep fear of lawyers.

We worked and worked and worked. I developed a new appreciation for anyone who has to clean up tiles and get the dirt out from inside all those little cracks in a tile floor.

We finally got it clean. That is, we got the floor clean and carpet clean. Unfortunately, we couldn't get the air clean!

Spray cleaner didn't do it. Air freshener didn't do it. We couldn't open up the window or the pipes would freeze. We settled on scented candles.

They worked, but we had to extinguish them when we left. Needless to say, we left the keys in the room. We also left out the side entrance.

I believe "quick checkout" was invented for times like this!

Then we left as quickly as we could. I let the dog out for a second time even though it didn't seem necessary. Like I said, Casey had nothing inside left to do.

I'm a little hesitant to write this story. I hope we don't still have legal liability for property destruction.

I was glad that our identification listed us as residents of Wisconsin. We probably ruined the reputation of the Badger State for generations to come. The motel couldn't have possibly known where we were going.

We finally made it to Rochester. Because of the terrible weather, we got there at night. The power was out there, too. Our wonderful new neighbors ran long extension cords from across the street so their generator would give us a little power.

Diane and I huddled under an electric blanket—on a bare mattress—to catch up on a little sleep.

After a while—several months actually—we were finally able to laugh about our cold trip to old New York.

Casey even wagged his tail about it.

CHAPTER 42

Bringing Katie Home

We were living in Rochester, New York. Four of our grandchildren came to visit. Hailli, Daniel, Sammy… and Katie.

As usual, like all grandchildren, they were awfully young and fantastically cute. Especially Katie. Just a little ray of sunshine all the time! We had a wonderful visit and then it was time to drive all of them back to Wisconsin. Off we went.

Since it was such a long drive with four young bladders, we decided to go only to near Cleveland and stay the night in a motel.

Unfortunately, while we were on a long and lonely stretch of Pennsylvania road at night, Katie had to go. I mean, really go! And not number one! We drove and drove and drove.

No exit, followed by even more no exits.

After a while, she started to really cry. "I gotta go! I gotta go!"

Well, what are you gonna do? A girl's gotta do what a girl's gotta do.

I was so glad Diane was along. We slid open the side door of our van and there Katie went. Sitting inside, going outside. We used Kleenex. Left it all there on the side of the road. If an outside toilet is good enough for the animals, it was good enough for us! I hoped.

Things didn't go much better when we reached a Cleveland suburb and decided to stop. It was so late. We didn't really have much choice of motels. We found one and reserved a room.

Everybody was happy except Katie. She had to go again. This time it *was* number one.

It took way too long to check in. I think the clerk had been asleep when we came in. There was no restroom in the lobby for Katie. She hopped and we hoped.

Finally, the clerk gave us a key and we drove around quickly to the room. Katie was desperate. We were all in a hurry.

Naturally, the key didn't fit the lock.

I can't believe we actually did this, but we sat her down on the curb of the parking lot, took off her underpants and she let fly! I didn't realize she was so healthy! It shot out like a cannon!

Diane and I thought she might be scarred for life. But Katie laughed like crazy. She thought it was the funniest thing ever! We didn't think it was all that great, but we went along with it. We didn't have too much choice, now did we?

I didn't really want to clean up the parking lot. Of course, it never rains when you want. Thank goodness for evaporation.

The other kids did potty stops where you're supposed to do them.

We knew that anything else happening from then on would be all right with us!

It was.

CHAPTER 43

Three Sleeping Truckers

I can personally verify that it's a long way from Wisconsin to New York.

For some reason, we made that trek an awful lot of times. It was longer to go see the boys at college in Texas, but we made that trip so often, our cars steered there automatically.

New York was a different story. It was a hard drive going back to Wisconsin and, for some reason, an even harder one driving back.

There was another problem.

Diane likes to occasionally "rest her eyes" when she's driving. Usually, this works out all right. She quickly opens them again. Or wakes up when the car tires hit the rumble strips on the side of the road.

But let's just say it's tough for me to sleep when she's sleeping... er, I mean, when she's driving.

Anyway, our friends in Wisconsin invited us to their son's wedding. It was on a Sunday afternoon. That would mean a long drive back to New York in the afternoon. Unfortunately, the church where I was on staff called an important meeting for 9:00 AM on Monday.

We'd have to drive all night.

Well, having never declined an invitation to anything in our entire marriage, we made plans. First, we decided to leave right after the wedding. Then we'd take turns driving all night. Diane would take over a little so I wouldn't be too tired for the Monday morning meeting. Sounds good, right?

The first part of the plan (leaving early) came up against a never-to-be-violated rule of nature. Diane never leaves early. Never ever. There are always other people to talk with, other new friends with which to get acquainted and, most often, at least thirty thousand more words to say.

I call it "procrastination." She calls it "relationships." Others would call it "insane," especially when you have to drive all the way back to New York right after the shindig.

We finally left. I drove. And drove. And drove.

Partly this was because I really wanted to get back for the meeting. But also, I drove for another reason. Diane was out like a light. Zonked. Sawing z's. Reading her eyelids. You get the picture.

She didn't wake up for five states.

Finally, I got tired. Seeing triple was my first clue. I woke her up. "Honey, I can't drive any more. I've got to rest."

She snapped to attention. "Great! I'm ready to go!"

Off we went. Her driving. I was so weary that I laid down in the back seat. I was asleep immediately, even though sardines in cans are probably more comfortable.

Diane, on the other hand, had relaxed considerably from her original "snap to attention." There were several roads on the highway in front of her and she got tired of trying to pick which one was right.

So she pulled off into a rest area. There were two trucks side by side. She pulled in between them and just behind another one in front. It was cold. To stay warm, the drivers had their engines running and their lights on.

Diane didn't want to wake me. She kept the car running. The heater blowing. The headlights still on. The radio playing softly.

Then she rested her eyes.

Unfortunately, I woke up. The car was running. We were in a real traffic jam between two trucks. She was tailgating a truck right in front of us. The radio was on. And Diane was asleep.

DIANE WAS ASLEEP!

"HONEY, WAKE UP! WE'RE GONNA DIE!"

She snapped to attention for another time.

After several of her rather incoherent explanations (it was hard for her to talk while sleeping), I calmed down.

No sleep possible now. I took over driving. Diane hadn't used up all of her thirty thousand words, so she talked with me the whole way to New York. She said it was to keep me from going to sleep.

No danger of that.

All along the way to New York, we didn't even blink.

The next morning—Monday—the meeting was cancelled.

CHAPTER 44

The Nightmare Was Worse Than the Surgery

One cold winter morning, I took the garbage cans out to the curb and slipped on the ice. I banged my head on the sidewalk. Harder than ever before.

Almost immediately, my left arm was engulfed in a white-hot flame of pain. I endured it for a while, but it only got worse. The result was four neck and spine surgeries. From which I am still recovering, years later.

One night at the hospital, I couldn't sleep. How does anyone ever sleep in a hospital with all those lights and beeping sounds? And if you ever *do* actually fall asleep, a perky nurse drops by to check your vitals, give you a shot or make you take a pill.

They do, however, courteously ask, "Are you awake?" I wonder if anyone ever says, "No."

By the way, if you ever need to have a shot, ask for an older nurse. They seem to have a better understanding of the concept of pain.

Older nurses sort of ease the needle in, then slowly inject the stuff. Younger nurses tend to stab you with it. Then they hit the end like a cowboy pushing the plunger on a dynamite detonator in an old Western movie.

If you get it in the rear, you'll remember it for a week every time you try to sit down.

But I digress…

Like I said, I couldn't sleep. The nurse suggested a sleep aid. I agreed. I had never taken one before. I had no idea what it would do. But I assumed it would help me sleep. It did.

For obvious reasons, the brand name shall forever remain a mystery.

Unfortunately, I am allergic to it. Deathly allergic to it. It gave me vivid, realistic, terrible dreams.

I proceeded to have the worst nightmare ever.

In my dream, I was caught up in some sort of hallway with a huge mob of people all trying to get out of somewhere. Unfortunately, there was a big light at the end of the hallway that was killing everybody.

I saw all the people dying as soon as they hit the light. Naturally, I struggled against the crowd, trying not to be swept along. I tried and tried.

Then I woke up. Or, I *thought* I woke up. Actually, I was still dreaming. In my dream, I got up from my bed and looked out into the hallway. Equipment and carts were strewn everywhere. And everyone was dead. Bodies everywhere. Patients, nurses, doctors.

So still in my dream, I went back into my room and laid down, terrified. Then I *really* woke up.

But I couldn't figure out what to do. Everyone was dead. How would I get help? Who would take care of me? The only thing I could think of was to take an elevator to another floor and see if there were any survivors.

Thank goodness I never actually made it to an elevator!

So I got up. Unfortunately, all my tossing and turning (and probably running in bed!) had left me wearing nothing but the catheter and a bunch of tubes.

I got up, dragging along my little tower with those wonderful little bags of hootch hanging from it.

I came out of my room, looking like death warmed over, and scared the poor nurse like she's never been scared in her life. Her skin was as white as her dress.

"What in the world!" she said. "John, why are you up?"

"I have to do something! *We* have to do something! Everybody is dead!" It all made sense to me except for one thing. Where were all the dead bodies and broken equipment all over the floor?

Another excellent question would have been, "How and why are you still alive?" However, like Adam and Eve after the apple, I was also slowly becoming aware of something else. I had been better dressed at birth.

"John," she said, in the greatest understatement in the entire history of the known universe, "I think you might be a little confused."

I suppose I *was* confused. If it's possible to be a little confused and tremendously terrified, that was me.

I was uncertain, unhappy, unpeaceful, and uh, undressed.

She gently guided me back to my bed. I didn't want to go. Dreams happen there.

The poor nurse kept reassuring me, "Don't worry, John. You're just a little confused." She was probably right, but wrong about the degree of my condition. I was even more confused than usual.

"Would you like me to give you something to help you go back to sleep... ?"

"Uh, no," I said. I wasn't *that* confused.

ABOUT THE AUTHOR

Rev. John Schmidtke lives in Milwaukee, Wisconsin, with Diane, his wife of nearly fifty years. They have four adult children and eighteen grandchildren. They live in a nice little house run by a spoiled-rotten pug-spaniel named Reggie. John is an ordained nondenominational minister and served in four churches. He has also been an entrepreneur, marketing executive, and public relations pro. He enjoys writing, laughing and not catching fish not necessarily in that order.

CPSIA information can be obtained
at www.ICGtesting.com
Printed in the USA
BVOW04s0818270517
485369BV00001B/74/P